1800 Kilometers in a FIAT 500

An Italian Genealogical Odyssey

by

Peter and Gayann Tricarico Barbella

Library of Congress Control Number 2014919951

ISBN-13: 978-1501027512

Table of Contents

This Book is dedicated to il miei amici:

Oreste Barbella
Veronica Barbella
Michele Cartusciello
Anna Michela
Pellegrino Mascolo
Francesco and Marie Mascolo
Don Otello Russo
Joe De Simone
Vito Tricarico
Domenico Tricarico
Marie Pedone
Anna Tricarico
Grazia Tricarico
Diego Sorice
Peter and Anna Ventresca
Bruna Bucciarelli & Bepe Robusto
Unidentified Clerk at the Vasto Ufficio di Anagrafe
Marie and Domenico Vero
Angela Lattanzio and Domenico Amendolara
The Trotta Brothers
And all others who helped bring our dream vacation to fruition

Prologue

If you are not a genealogist or you are not keen on travel in Italy, put this book down right now. Go and find yourself a novel to read. If you fail to take this advice, you will be making a huge mistake. You see, genealogy is more addictive than any drug could ever be, and if you get caught in its iron grip, it will cost you your time and your sanity not to mention a good deal of your money.

"Travel in Italy" can do likewise. Italy is so rich in antiquity that you cannot come away without increased knowledge of its history, and a longing to know more. You cannot journey through Italy without gaining an appreciation for the enormous role this country has played in the development and genealogy of European man.

There is nothing strange about the bedfellows, genealogy and history. Wherever you look, they walk hand in hand. But, make no mistake, genealogy (and travel) have an enormous power to entice. So, if you are not a travel loving genealogist, drop the book now, walk away quietly, and no one gets hurt.

If you are an adventurous genealogist, or you lack the wisdom to heed our advice, this book will take you on a thirteen day magical genealogy trip through the lower half of the Italian peninsula, Italy's so called mezzogiorno. You are about to go to places that Rick Steeves has likely never seen. The book stars two people who have already been entrapped by this most insidious hobby; my wife and I.

Gay and Pete; two people who long to know more about their families and the land from which they came. Read on and we are going to take you to places you have never heard of. We will not dance with Luigi[1], but we will dance with fireflies. We will dance with Vito and Pellegrino, and Don Otello Russo and a few more.

The book begins with our personal introduction to genealogy. We fell into a genealogical rabbit hole unlike anything Lewis Carroll's Mad Hatter ever had to encounter. It describes our early genealogical findings which drove us to an absolutely unquenchable thirst for more. It attempts to find words to express just how satisfying it was, and still is, to discover new data about the people in our families and learn about some of their history.

Genealogy is a pastime/hobby/avocation which has the power to consume your thoughts. It introduces you to people that you never knew and many that you never will know and, at the same time, when done properly, it leads you, inextricably, to facts which reveal the lives of these people in ways that you never thought were possible. Here is how we fell into genealogy's trap.

Our Beginning

The Mayflower – The American Revolution

We entered the genealogical world in a somewhat serendipitous manner. We discovered that Gay's mother

---

1   Paolicelli, Paul. "Dances with Luigi", St. Martins Griffin, 2001

had Irish and English roots that led directly to the
Mayflower and the Revolutionary War. This past revealed
some very interesting characters and some riveting
American stories which literally jumped out at us from our
computers.

It all started over dinner with friends.

Phil Keane is an avid genealogist, and one day we were
sitting at the dinner table discussing ancestors. Gay
showed Phil a genealogy book that we had hardly ever
looked at. It had been a gift from her cousin, the late
Robert Tomonto. Bob used to pester us constantly for the
latest family information and he was continuously gifting
us with books and digital CD's loaded with genealogical
information.

Phil looked the information over with great interest. He
leafed through the pages slowly with an occasional
"hmm". Finally he raised his eyebrows as though he had
discovered gold, lifted his head out of the book and
proclaimed that he and Gay were cousins. They were both
descendants of Richard Warren, a Mayflower passenger.

Gay wasn't sure what to think about this revelation, but
she liked the thought of being descended from a line of the
original Pilgrims. All of a sudden her nose lifted a little
higher and she sat up a little straighter and wanted to look
at the books and CDs which she had never opened in the
three or four years since cousin Bob had given them to us.

Thus began a journey to membership into the National

Society of Mayflower Descendants. It also revealed that Gay had Revolutionary War ancestors which led her into the Daughters of the American Revolution. Phil encouraged Gay to apply for these memberships, and she did.

The requirements to membership in these societies were straightforward, however they required organization and compilation of a number of records we did not have. The computer skills required to do the searching and recording were more up my line, so, I reluctantly joined Gay in the hunt, and together, we began to study and compile records of her English and Dutch ancestors.

Our findings were based on Gay's maternal relatives, the Hammonds and Kittles. To our astonishment, we were able to uncover an incredible number of facts and documents which revealed the fascinating stories of Archelaus Hammond[2] and Willem Kettel.

The Italians

So, with this work under our belts, we both felt like we were becoming genuine genealogists. We had made numerous findings. We had traveled to historic societies in Southeastern Massachusetts. We visited the town of Mattapoisett. Here we walked the grounds of the Hammond Cemetery. We went to Albany, New York, and to Schaghticoke, NY in search of Kettel records of the

2   See, for example, Leonard, Mary Hall. "Mattapoisett and Old Rochester Massachusetts", Grafton Press, 1907, or www.nonoandpapa.com/Hammond History.

"Great Schaghticoke Indian Massacre[3].

The facts we uncovered came so fast and fascinated us so intensely that we were in danger of proceeding, with blinders, along the "American-only" line. One day, it dawned on us that we were ignoring the other 75% of our parents, the Italians. We began to wonder about the Barbellas, the Tricaricos, and the Mascolos. It was fairly easy finding data and facts about Gay's Dutch and English early settlers of America's 17th century. It would be another matter to begin uncovering facts about immigrants from Italy who were relative newcomers to this land. We were about to enter a different world.

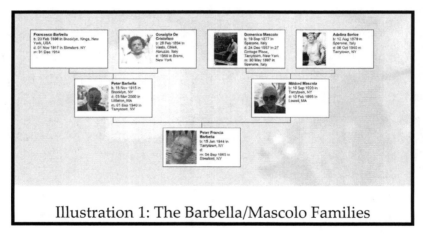

Illustration 1: The Barbella/Mascolo Families

As we thought more and more about our Italian ancestors, I began thinking much more about my own Dad's family.

Here was a real mystery. I never knew my paternal grandfather. Francesco Barbella, who was born in

---

3   See, for example, "The Ketel Family", by Sumner Eli Wetmore Kitelle, 1946

America, and died when my Dad was only two years old.
I didn't know enough about Dad's family to fill a thimble.
As luck would have it, Dad had passed on several years
before I got curious. To make matters worse, he left me a
bag full of photographs, none of which were captioned. I
could identify only a few of the people in the photos. How
frustrating was this?

I knew a little more about Mom's family. We lived with
them when I was young. I personally knew Grandpa
Mascola and I knew my several aunts and uncles. Mom
never talked much about her natural mother, who died
before I was born. I knew Grandpa was an accomplished

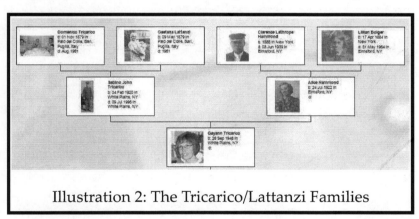

Illustration 2: The Tricarico/Lattanzi Families

stone mason who had built many of the stone structures in
my hometown, Tarrytown, New York. The Mascola family
got together many times during my childhood, but rarely
would the conversation include stories about the old
country. Most of my aunts and uncles were born in the
United States.

Gay knew about as much of her father's family as I did of

my mother's. She had actually known her grandmother, Gaetana Lattanzi, and even I had met her grandfather, Domenico. We knew they hailed from a place called Palo del Colle.

So it is that we began anew to study our immigrant ancestors, and the Italian language and Italian records and so on and so forth. We started with the Barbella family. I uncovered a marriage certificate from my Dad's papers. The marriage was between Cecelia DeCristofaro and Francesco Barbella, Dad's natural parents. We found that Cecelia was born in a place named Vasto to Raffaele DeCristofaro and Maria Trivelli, and that Francesco's father and mother were Pietro Barbella and Francesca Galatro.

Later I found a passport application for Pietro Barbella. Apparently he was bringing his son Francesco and his daughter, Antonia to Italy. It gave his birth date and home town, Sassano, in Italy's Salerno province.

I quickly ordered the available civil records[4] of Sassano from the Latter Day Saints (LDS) microfilm library in Salt Lake City, and, sure enough, I found Pietro's birth certificate. What a thrill. There it was, just as it had stated on the passport application, January 31, 1867.

Fresh from that success, we ordered more LDS microfilms, this time for Sperone and for Vasto and for Palo del Colle. With a large investment in time, we uncovered various records of our families, all the way back to the early 1700s.

---

4   Years ago the Latter Day Saints photographed millions of civil records throughout Europe and made them available to researchers.

These records helped us to begin to understand the stories of the people who came before us.

The discoveries we made came, at first, with blinding speed. But soon, the discoveries took longer and longer to make, and we quickly realized that new discoveries would come only from records waiting for us in Italy.

Italy! That is an expensive proposition. We could not possibly think of traveling across the ocean until we have exhausted every avenue of research available to us, here, in the states, could we?

Enough is Enough -Time to Visit Italy

We continued our research. We examined records and we studied Italian history. We traced our immigrants into this country and found how their families grew and prospered. We found cousins in California we had not previously known.

As time passed, we kept adding little bits and pieces. Yet, as time passed, it became increasingly clear that new "old" information was getting harder and harder to find. We began corresponding with Italian archives[5] to try to uncover more data. Through numerous emails, written in Italian, we made yet a few more discoveries, however, we came to the realization that the really old records, pre-

---

5   Virtually every Italian province has an archive which houses thousands of government records. These include, but are not limited to births, marriages and deaths. In each province, the archive for each province is known as the Archivio di Stato.

Napoleonic records, would only be found in the local churches of the towns our ancestors came from.

Discovery of old records became rarer and rarer. The consequence of this was that the value of a trip to Italy was becoming greater and greater. It was clear that we were going to have to travel if we wanted to discover more information. While we may not have exhausted 100% of the records available to us, here in the states, enough was enough! In our minds, the value of the trip now exceeded its cost. It was time to go to Italy.

We made that trip to Italy and that's what this book is all about. On our way we made new friends and many discoveries, of history as well as of genealogy. We made a very thorough plan and we executed that plan as best we could. We had a few failures and a number of successes.

In the end, we came away with enormous satisfaction. This was indeed an odyssey to remember and we hope that you enjoy reading about our adventures. We hope you get some ideas for yourselves, learn from our mistakes, and, somehow, benefit from our successes.

So fasten your seat-belts and hold on to your chairs. We are about to begin a thirteen day whirlwind tour of southern Italy.

1800 Kilometers in a FIAT 500

Getting to Rome

The big day is here. There is no turning back now. It is time to fly to Rome. It is Friday evening, April 25, 2014 and we are about to board an airplane at Logan International Airport. The airplane is going to fly all night, and then land in Rome around noon on the next day. In addition to that, there's a six hour time warp so I'm not at all sure that when we land, I am going to be up to driving a rental car from Rome to Naples. Neither of us sleeps well on an airplane, and that is not going to be helpful. But this is the plan and, somehow, we will have to make it work.

We've packed our passports and our wad of Euros in our body pouches tucked neatly away inside our shirts where pickpockets will have to denude us to get them. The bags were all packed and waiting in a straight line at the front door. All the electronic devices were stowed away and we were ready to go. Pat, our son-in-law kindly agreed to provide our "limo" service to the airport. When he drove into the driveway to pick us up, we were ready to go.

The ride to the airport was swift and uneventful, with little traffic to contend with. Our only worry was the nagging suspicion that we had forgotten something. I suspect that this is a common apprehension among travelers.

When we got to Logan airport, there was much hustle and bustle at the International terminal. We thanked Pat for his kind help as we unloaded the car, and we rolled our bags towards the Alitalia counter.

Getting our large bags checked was a piece of cake. But the next stop was security and this three ring circus was in a state of pandemonium. The best way to describe it is that there were 1000 people in a ten people line. After what seemed like an hour, we had inched our way up to the X-ray machine.

I dutifully removed my shoes, opened my computers, and removed all metallic items from my pants pocket. Unfortunately, I left a handkerchief in my pocket and unbeknownst to me, this was a no no. That blunder got me singled out for a more thorough search. By the time I got through the security line, I felt as though I had just worked an 8 hour day. However, we made it through, and we had a good hour to wait for our flight.

We found a seat at the gate, and tried to relax for a few minutes. It didn't work. Perhaps the physical act of relaxing was taking place. We were sitting down. Mental relaxation, however, was simply not happening. Over and over again, questions kept running through our minds. "What in the world are we doing here?". Were we really about to attempt to drive a car in Italy, south, east, north, and west? During this eight hour flight are we going to be cramped up like human pretzels, or would there be room for our legs in these very expensive seat upgrades? Aren't we simply too old to be doing what we are trying to do?

Are we crazy?

Illustration 3: Relaxing (?) at the gate

Andiamo a Roma

Eventually our flight was called and we boarded the plane.
To my relief, there was ample room for our overhead bags
and the seat was quite roomy. It was not first class, but
there was room for me to stretch my legs and keep my
ailing knees from cramping up on me. The seats reclined
to a fairly comfortable position. Maybe this was going to
be alright.

We had great service on the flight, including a
dinner/snack. It was late and we had eaten a meal before
coming to the airport, but being in an airplane has the
peculiar effect of creating a voracious appetite, so we
enjoyed the meal.

Illustration 4: It was expensive, but, in the end, I think the business class seats were worth it.

I had a little opportunity to practice some Italian with the attendants and there was a nice selection of movies and other entertainment to watch.   Even so, I tend to want to simply view the little map which shows where the airplane is and how much more there is to go. I guess I never outgrew that "are we there yet?" mentality.

We managed to get a little sleep on the aircraft thanks to the slightly more comfortable seats. In the morning, the crew served a nice breakfast as they gently woke us up just prior to landing. The landing was smooth, but not as smooth as the passport inspection. I don't think the agent even bothered to look at us, and the line was not long at all.

The customs check was another matter. When we got off

the plane, there was only a small line to pass through. It appeared to be another cakewalk. This check was separated into two lines, and both lines were moving along nicely processing the people who were on our flight.

Gay chose this time to take a bathroom break. While she was there, another plane must have landed because all of a sudden there was an enormous hoard of people heading for the two available lines to the passport check

I did not want to get stuck in a long line so I hurriedly walked away from the ladies room entrance and got onto one of the two lines to beat the crowd. I didn't see the sign which said that this particular line was for Italian citizens only. I was too busy looking frantically for Gay.

I reached a point where I could go no further without her so I began letting one passenger after another cut in front of me. I needed her **NOW**, but she was not there. Finally she appeared and, of course, I was not where she was expecting me to be.

I waved excitedly and finally got her attention. She joined me and we proceeded until we found out that we were in the wrong line. At that point, we sheepishly crossed underneath a line barrier and slithered into the correct line, all the time feeling the malocchi (evil eyes) of all the people we were cutting in front of. Other than that, the passport check was a breeze.

The customs check was simpler and easier than the passport check. I'm not sure anyone cared what we were bringing into the country.

When we got into the baggage return area, there were already bags coming around on the turntable. People from our flight were crowded around the nearest turnstile, but no one was retrieving a bag.

Since the flight number posted on this turnstile did not correspond with our flight, I wandered down the hall looking for an alternate carousel with our flight number. After four more carousels, I finally found the one which listed our flight. At this point, Gay was not in sight, but I figured she couldn't be far behind me; could she? There were now hundreds of people all around the carousels.

After a while, our two large bags came out and I picked them off the turntable and looked for Gay. She was still nowhere in sight. She couldn't still be at the first turnstile, could she? I've been married long enough to know that what can't be usually is. So, I started to make my way back towards her last verifiable position, scanning the crowd and kicking myself for not remembering what colors she was wearing.

Do you think it is easy wheeling two large bags and one carry-on simultaneously through a crowded airport baggage area? It is not. But, I made my way slowly. I was beginning to panic. There was no sign of her. I began thinking about how I would describe my wife to the Italian Pollizioto. Where is she?

I continued down the hall, finally getting close enough to

the first turnstile to spot Gay, still there looking for our bags. After some frantic waving and hollering, I got her attention and we were united once again, with baggage in hand. Grazie di Dio! We were ready for our next task.

Where's Avis?

That next task was to find the Avis car rental counter and get our reserved BMW. We were looking forward to riding in our first BMW. But finding the auto rental counter turned out to be not so simple a task which resulted in a major change to our plan.

Illustration 5: Fiumicino Airport, Rome, April 26, 2014 – Where are the auto rental counters?

I've done a lot of domestic traveling in my working career. In any American airport, while you are waiting for your bags to arrive on the carousel, you can look around and see a long row of car rental counters, usually within a few hundred feet of where you're standing. Not so, here at Fiumicino in Rome. Not only can you not see a car rental counter, you cannot see a sign directing you to any car rental counters.

So we began to walk along the main corridor towards the airport exit, all the time expecting to run into a sign pointing towards the car rental areas. There was nothing!

We began to think that, just maybe, you have to go outside and board a shuttle bus. I stopped at an information booth to ask. I was told to walk past the main exit, down a long corridor and take the escalator up two floors. Did I understand this man correctly? Could the car rental counters really be that far away from the baggage area?

Trusting this man, we walked down the long corridor and took the escalator up, as directed, and still there were no signs to the "autonoleggio"(car rental). With a little panic setting in I asked another attendant the same question and he said we had to go through the double doors and walk down the next hall. This hall was a little more than a quarter mile long. Mercifully there was an automated walkway to traverse the distance quickly, but still, I'm thinking, "Who puts the car rental counters this far from the passengers?" Just maybe someone might be telling us it's a bad idea to rent a car in Italy.

When we got to the end of this hallway, we finally found a sign pointing to the rental counters. Gay sat down for a much needed rest and I approached the Avis counter. I discovered that I needed to take a ticket, which I did. To my disbelief, I had ticket number 74 and they were working on ticket number 49. What? Well, perhaps it will go quickly (NOT!). This happened to be a very busy day in Rome. It was the day before the canonization of two popes at the Vatican. Half the Catholic world was here to attend the canonization of popes John XXIII and John Paul II. I think they were all at the Avis counter. After a half hour wait, they were on ticket 57.

At this point, I took another ticket; this time from the Hertz counter. They seemed to be moving much quicker and I had a hunch I would get out of town quicker if I made the switch. My hunch paid off. My Hertz number was up while Avis was still working number 64. This was a long shot because I did not have a reservation with Hertz, but I figured it was worth a try.

I approached the counter and sheepishly announced that even though I had no Hertz reservation, would it still be possible to rent a car from Hertz today? I was relieved when they said yes, I could have a FIAT 500 with room for 5 passengers and 3 large bags.

A FIAT what? What was that going to be like? I sighed as I thought about the BMW we were giving up. That's what I had reserved at Avis, but we were really anxious to get out of town. It's never good when your emotions cloud your brain, but that is a Barbella genetic defect which we must live with. I made the switch. (We were not disappointed.)

Reluctantly, I agreed to rent the smaller and more mundane FIAT 500. Even though I was a little apprehensive about the leg room in a FIAT, we were so ready to be out of the airport and on the road to get this adventure going.

Now I had a major navigation option to decide upon. I could equip my vehicle with a GPS or, for half the price, I could rent a small device which would give us a mobile internet connection throughout Italy. Hertz, of course, wanted me to take both, but they did not realize that, with internet, we knew how to use our mobile phone as a GPS.

With only a little thought, I saved big bucks by refusing the GPS and taking the WIND Mobile internet device only.

Finally, I got my keys and my magic internet device and we were off to find the car. That was only two floors below and a walk down another long hall. When I reached the numbered parking spot, there was our four door FIAT 500, a little mini SUV. Spotless white, the car looked brand new. We opened the back hatch and got three of our four bags in. The last bag went comfortably into the back seat.

I got into the drivers seat and adjusted it all the way to the rear. To my relief, there was enough leg room for me to handle the gas, clutch, and brake. The FIAT had an unmistakable smell of a brand new car. I looked over the five speed transmission with just a little fear. I can't remember the last time I drove a standard transmission vehicle. I checked out the wipers and the lights. I beeped the horn and tried the turn signals. This was going to be an exciting experiment.

Illustration 6: The FIAT 500

Now it was time to make our internet connection. We took out the internet device, and, as promised, with the push of a button, we were connected. I took our smart phone and set it into GPS mode. I programmed our first destination, in the small village of Quadrelle and, with adrenalin flowing, we were ready to roll.

Ok Italy, here we come. Are you ready for us, Avellino?

We fired up the FIAT. The diesel engine kicked over and our next task was to locate the exit from the garage. The exit was clearly marked and before you could say "mozzarella," we were on our way.

Out on the airport plaza, the phone began barking orders at us to turn this way or that, generally doing a fine job at finding the road which would lead us out of Rome. We wanted to get out of the city as quickly as we could because the roads were very busy. The combination of timely commands from the phone GPS and well marked roads resulted in an easy exit.

We managed to make our way out of town with only one near crash, a dozen or so Italian horns, and at least a few hundred malocchi. The next thing we knew, we were on the AutoStrada, heading for Naples. The telephone GPS was working like a charm.

With small sighs of relief, we settled into our comfortable seats. Could this be real? I had to pinch myself to believe we had made it this far in our dream trip. At the same time, we realized that we had only just begun. There was a lot of adventure to come, and it was going to come, perhaps, a little quicker than we were hoping for.

Time For Lunch and Our First Major Problem

After getting safely out of Rome, we took a few deep breaths and, despite the constant drizzle, began enjoying the Italian countryside. Soon, we decided it was time to have a little lunch. We pulled into the first Auto-Grill[6] that

---

6   Italian Auto-Grills are an upgrade to the frequent rest stops on American highways. They feature fresh local foods as well as a variety of products. Of course, if you want, you can also get

we encountered. In the store, the food section contained
an enormous selection of salads, pasta dishes, calzones and
pizzas. We selected a few pieces of a very different looking
pizza and a few soft drinks. We ate our food at a small
table and then browsed the other merchandise in the store.
People were coming and going in droves, proving that
Saturday must be a busy day on the AutoStrada. We left
the store, got into the FIAT and continued our journey
towards Naples.

Illustration 7: The rainy road to Naples

After a mile or two, the sky became a little more overcast
and the rain fell at a steady rate. Driving along, we noticed
that our phone GPS application was strangely silent. I
began to wonder about this unusual lack of commands. It
was more than a little discomforting.

---

gasoline there.

I found a place to pull over so that we could take a good look at the equipment to be sure we were still connected. The first thing I saw was that the smart phone was no longer connected to the internet. Hmm! The second thing I noticed was that the "magic" internet box that cost me 150 euros at Hertz was displaying a red marker, perhaps indicating no connection. Great! What should I do now? There was only one button on the WIND Mobile internet device, so I used it. I continually powered it off and on over and over again in an attempt to reset the electronics, but still, there was no connection to the internet. Try as I might, the marker remained red.

This was clearly not good. Here we are in Italy with no maps and a non functioning internet device. Now we wished that we had taken that GPS that Hertz was trying to rent us. We knew that we needed to turn east about 20 Km north of Naples. This would get us going in the direction of Avellino. Since we were still about 60 Km north of Naples, we decided to drive on and think about our options.

We were angry with ourselves for not having a back-up plan for this situation. We were the victims of overconfidence in technology. If only we had purchased a good old fashioned map, we might better know when to get off the highway and how to proceed. Without electronics or a map, we were totally blind.

As we approached Naples, we found a convenient place to pull over and strategize. Our first stop was to the home of Joe DeSimone, an English speaking genealogist from the small commune of Quadrelle, near Avellino. We had Joe's phone number, so I gave him a call to enlist his aid. After explaining our dilemma to Joe, he had a solution to our predicament.

Joe was happy to hear that we had arrived in Italy safely and he gave us some instructions to get us closer to our destination. He told us what exit to use to get off the AutoStrada. Then he gave us directions to the intersection of two major highways. When and if we got there we could simply give him another call and he would come and escort us to his home.

Illustration 8: The arranged meeting place

His plan worked, kind of. We got a lot closer to Quadrelle, but then I became confused. I could not find the intersection that Joe had mentioned. Feeling sure that we were a lot closer than before, we pulled off the highway, and gave Joe a second call. When we described our surroundings, he knew exactly where we were and with a few more simple instructions, he directed us to a gas station just a few miles away. He said we couldn't miss it because there was an airplane mounted on a pole right next to it. We went as directed, found the airplane, and, with high confidence, waited.

Illustration 9: Our kitchen at casa di Joe Simone

After a few minutes had passed, Joe drove into the lot. It didn't take him long to scan the people in the parking lot and pick out the lost Americani. We simply were the most forlorn looking people there. We introduced ourselves and thanked Joe for rescuing us. Then we got into our car and followed Joe a short distance, back to his home. If I can say so myself, we did quite well keeping that FIAT close to a real Italian driver and not getting ourselves lost again.

With Joe leading the way, we drove to his lovely home on a narrow street in the commune of Quadrelle. The street was lined with houses on small lots, and parking was at a premium. We parked the FIAT in front and Joe led us into our very spacious quarters on the first level of his two level house. We met his wife, Maria and we moved our bags in. This is going to be home for the next few days and were we ever glad to be here, at our first stop, after our long day of travel.

We sat and chatted for a while about our plans to visit the nearby communes of Sperone and Avella to see the home towns of the Mascolos and the Sorices. Joe informed us that Pellegrino Mascolo had called earlier, inquiring about our arrival. Pellegrino is a Facebook friend with a potential connection to my mother's family. We have communicated on the computer and on the telephone in the past, and he knew we were coming to Quadrelle. It was nice to hear that he had inquired but we weren't sure anything would come of this.

We knew that no public office would be open on Sunday, but our original plan included researching some records at the local regional archdiocese. Joe put a damper on those plans by informing us that the local archdiocese, Nola, was closed until September. Plan B was to relax a little and do some sightseeing, and visit some family churches.

At this point, it was about 6:00 PM on Saturday evening in Italy, or noon back in Boston. We were hoping to make our mass obligation on Saturday, but it was too late to make an evening mass, so we arranged to attend mass with Joe and his wife in Quadrelle the next day, Sunday. We were, strangely, not hungry, so, being thoroughly tired, we decided to simply crash and start anew on Sunday. After seventeen hours of travel, crash we did. The beginning of our genealogical touring can wait until tomorrow, Sunday.

Sperone and Avella

In the morning, Joe knocked on the door early. He wanted to take us for a ride to see a few of the local churches that were likely prominent in the lives of the Mascolo and Sorice ancestors. In particular, we had, via email, previously discussed the church of San Marino. Despite the fact that this church had long ago changed its name to San Giovanni, Joe knew where it was and wanted to show it to us.

Illustration 10: Chiesa di San Elia

Since I was ready to go, and Gay was still freshening up, Joe and I set off on our own. We only had a few minutes before the Sunday service we were all going to attend, so we needed to move quickly. This was going to be a quick tour.

Joe gave me a first lesson in Italian driving technique. It seems that whenever you approach an intersection from which another car is waiting or entering, you must automatically sound your horn to announce that you are coming through. OK! I'll have to try this in Boston.

Illustration 11: Hand crafted artifacts

We drove a short distance and stopped at the church of Saint Elia in the village of Sperone. Saint Elia (Elijah) is located on a small piazza, and almost looks more like a monument than a church, but looks are deceiving, and inside, we found far more than just a church despite the exterior size.

Joe explained to me that, in Italy, it was common to find churches open only when a mass was being celebrated. To our surprise, despite the fact that there was no mass scheduled for at least a few hours, the doors to Saint Elia were open. We found a custodian inside and he allowed us to come in and see the church.

Illustration 12: 15th Century Altar at Saint Elia Church in Sperone

Joe explained that there were actually two churches here. The large door in front of the church entered into the main, more modern church, and off to the right, a set of stairs led us down to another older section of the church which was originally constructed in the 1400s. This lower church is still in use. Along the left side of the lower church there was a labyrinth of side rooms devoted to antique displays and several nativity scenes.

Joe showed me a wall display of silver artifacts. He explained that each artifact was hand crafted by local people as an offering to Saint Elia, usually in thanks for some miraculous gift that they had received . For example, there were several heart shaped artifacts crafted by people who believed that prayer had cured their heart disease. There was a silver leg, crafted by someone whose leg had been healed. This wall display is a testament to the importance of religion in the lives of Italians past.

Illustration 13: Lower Church at Saint Elijah in Sperone

It is hard to describe what it is like to be in the presence of something that was created in the 15th century. This altar and these displays are nearly 600 years old. Today, we build things and if they last for 50 years we think it's a miracle. How did these people build, maintain and preserve this altar. I was struck with the amazing symmetry about the faded painting of Saint Elia. I wondered how many Mascolo and Sorice baptisms Saint Elia had looked down upon through the years. How blessed was I to be standing here witnessing this marvel of antiquity?

While this was not the most ornate altar we had ever seen, it had an innate beauty in its simplicity. The subdued shadows along the left side of the church were a striking contrast to the light from the windows shining on the right side which formed them. The same could be said of the orange glow cast along the ceiling by the circular stained glass window.

Illustration 14: Ancient tools and implements

Joe next led me down a side corridor in the lower church which led to a series of halls. The halls led to several rooms which contained a number of unique displays. The popularity of Christmas was evident because there were several Nativity scenes. There were also several displays of antique tools and implements. All of these displays were what I would call museum quality.

As we walked out of The "Chiesa di San Elia", I was already satisfied with our trip. It was worth the time and money just to see a single place where my ancestors had walked. This day had already fulfilled my expectations. But there was more to come; much much more. Joe next drove me to the church of San Marino.

Illustration 15: Nativity scene at the church of Saint Elia

I had first noticed the name of the Church of San Marino in the village of Avella on a Mascolo wedding record. It was the 1831 marriage of my great great grandparents, Domenico Mascolo and Paola Del Latte. I had been previously told, by Facebook friend, Pellegrino Mascolo, that there was no such church in Avella. Joe disagreed and we drove the car a very short distance into the neighboring village of Avella where he made his point.

I should point out that Avella and Sperone are two small villages, within a stone's throw of each other. Joe was not surprised that my ancestors have records from both communities. In fact, he explained that at one point in history, they were one commune, Avella. Sperone became its own village in the 19th century.

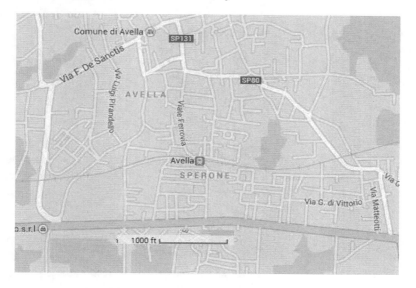

Illustration 16: Sperone and Avella

In any event, Joe drove me to the "Parrocchia di S. Marina, Collegiata di S. Giovanni". Literally, the church of Saint Giovanni which used to be the church of San Marino.

Illustration 17: Chiesa di San Marino

Here, again, was another magnificent find, however, this time, the church was closed. We would not be able to see the inside of this church.

I was astonished at the height of the door. Standing nearly twenty feet high, the door on this church was imposing. Obviously some very tall statues were processed in and out of this parish.

Illustration 18: Front of the church of San Marino

We lingered for a short while at the church. We met an elderly woman who was curious about why we were taking pictures of the church. It turns out that she knew the Mascolo name. She couldn't point out any nearby homes, but she knew the name. It was getting late, so we went back to Joe's place to pick up the ladies and go to Sunday mass in Quadrelle.

At the appointed hour, we all piled into Joe's car and drove to his local church for our Sunday service. Maria, Joe's wife, sang in the church choir and the remarkable acoustics in the church made the choir sound much larger than it actually was. Although there were no more than a dozen ladies in the choir, you would have thought there were 200 ladies on the altar singing together.

Initially, we had concerns that we might not be able to follow the basic parts of the mass. It was not clear that the Italian mass would be similar to the American mass. Our fears were unfounded. We had very little trouble recognizing the different parts of the mass, despite the prayers being in Italian. Thanks to Rosetta Stone, I even understood some of the homily.

Illustration 19: Perhaps this is where the Jolly Green Giant goes to church

We thoroughly enjoyed this mass. It was one of the goals of our trip; to mix with the people of Italy and enjoy their company away from any tourism. Here, at this mass our mission was, at least partially, accomplished. The church was beautiful, but, as you may realize, they don't believe in cushioned kneelers in Italy. Just the same, with minimal damage to our knees, we managed to "tough it out" and ended up enjoying the mass completely.

When we got back, Joe was gracious enough to loan us his GPS. He was concerned about us driving about town without some assistance. He mounted it in the FIAT for us and gave us some quick instructions on how to program it. Joe was sure that my language skills were sufficient to understand the instructions spoken in Italian. I did know most of the necessary words. We immediately nicknamed the female voice in the GPS, Sophia.

With a GPS installed in the FIAT, we were ready to strike out on our own. The first order of business was a little Sunday brunch.

Illustration 20: A new friend and parking lot attendant

We drove down a few side streets to the main drag in town and began driving towards Sperone. We found a little cafe and pulled into a side street. We were a little uncomfortable parking the car here as the road was very narrow and we were afraid that we might be taking up someone's private parking spot. There was a older gentleman standing in the street and I approached him to ask if it was OK to park there. I explained that we were Americans and that we were here to find records for the Mascolo and Sorice families.

Illustration 21: Very Narrow Streets in the old town

When I mentioned those names, his eyes lit up in recognition. He shook my hand vigorously. He knew the family names well. "Of course it would be OK to park here," he said and he promised to watch the car for us. Now I had a parking space and a security guard.
We entered the little cafe (or Bar as they are called in Italy) and we each ordered a small pastry and a cup of coffee. I have a very strong opinion of Italian coffee, espresso, but I'll try to keep most of that opinion to myself. I will provide only a brief critique here.

In short, I love Italy. I love all things Italian. I love the Italian people. I love everything there is about Italy, with one glaring exception. I can't imagine a nation of people who would drink a cup of Italian coffee for some type of culinary pleasure. In my opinion, the taste of Italian coffee is very close to Australian vegemite, which happens to be on my list of the top ten worst things to place in your mouth. I certainly can understand why it is served in such a small cup. No one could drink an entire mug of this stuff and live. It is likely much better suited for rubbing on bald heads to promote hair growth. Nevertheless, we politely sipped at our coffee, trying to feign normalcy. The coffee certainly made the pastry taste extra delicious.

After our brunch, we settled our bill, thanked our parking attendant and drove in the general direction of Sperone.

Illustration 22: The cemetery in Sperone

We came upon the local cemetery and lingered there for a few moments even though it was Sunday and the gates were closed. This was our first, but not last, look at an Italian cemetery. As I looked at the lines and lines of crypts, I tried to imagine how one would execute the Italian custom of managing cemeteries. Apparently, each

body is allowed to remain in the cemetery for only a fixed
number of years. After that, the remains are removed to an
ossuary to make room for other bodies.

I wouldn't relish that job. How could you open a crypt and
remove remains? I don't know if you could pay me
enough to do that. What procedure would they follow?
Would you open every crypt on a particular day of the
year and throw out anyone who has been in there for X
number of years? Or would you keep records of
everyone's stay and remove them on their anniversary
dates as needed? Talk about a morbid occupation.

Illustration 23: Gay in Avella to see the Chiesa di San Marino

I put these macabre thoughts away as we continued our
sight seeing tour through some impossibly narrow streets.
It was evident that the streets we were on were likely
hundreds of years old. You could see it in the look of the

stone and stucco. I wondered if my grandfather had laid any of these streets or put up any of the masonry walls. We continued back to the churches that Joe had taken me to earlier in the morning. I wanted Gay to see them.

We parked the car and walked over to the San Marino church again. It was still closed. Joe's words came back to haunt us. It is difficult to find a church open outside of mass time.

We drove around the towns of Sperone and Avella taking in one sight after the other. We engaged a few of the locals in conversation. Since it was near 2:00 PM, we were looking for a place to have lunch and most of the people we talked to looked at us strangely when we inquired about places to eat. After all, this was Sunday. What do you expect. Nothing is open. In fact, it is likely that there were no restaurants, at all, in this small town.

Eventually the two wandering Americani drove closer to Quadrelle to find a place on the main drag called the American Bar. Joe had mentioned that it was a fairly good place, and, as a bonus, when we got there it was open.

One narrow parking spot was all that we could find along the street. We took it, although we were not quite sure of its legality. As we got out of the car, two tiny dogs began barking at us from, thankfully, behind a fence. I suppose they were unhappy about us taking this spot which, I'm sure, belonged to their master.

Upon entering the Bar, we found several people smoking. That was not a good start. Neither of us can stand the smell of cigarette smoke, so we found a nice table outside, away from the smokers. The cafe had a wide selection of Italian treats. The cigarette smoke was not dense enough to keep us from marveling at the array of fresh calzones, pizzas, and pasta dishes. Although I wanted a cup of coffee, my better judgment kicked in and I ordered some

Illustration 24: Ricotta and Salami in a pastry shell - unbelievable

soda pop to go along with a few calzone type things with meat and cheese. There was no sign telling us the name of these calzones, but I could tell we were going to enjoy them no matter what they were called. Then I spotted a tart that looked very very interesting. It reminded me of something my mother used to make for us so long ago. It turned out to be even better than what I was remembering.

Filled with ricotta cheese and chunks of salami, it looked

extraordinarily good. Its ingredients were not what you
might think would be in a dessert, but I bought one
anyway. After we ate our calzones, we cut up the tart and
shared it.

The pastry was indescribably delicious. I couldn't believe
how good this was. I was sure I had died and gone to
heaven. We finished the tart and looked at each other.
There was no mistake about the silent communication
passing between us, with eyes alone. No word had to be
uttered. I got up, went back to the counter and bought two
more of these tarts and wrapped them up for a future
need. We drove back to Joe's home, and if it hadn't have
been for Gay, the tarts would not have survived the half
mile trip.

Pellegrino Mascolo, a Surprise Visit

When we got back to the apartment, Joe came down the
stairs and knocked on the door to tell us that he had
received a call from Pellegrino Mascolo who was inquiring
about us. He wanted to come for a visit.

Pellegrino is a young man that we connected with on social
media. We had several conversations with him on the
computer. He had shown a little interest in the possibility
that we might be related. We even arranged a phone call
one day when his English speaking friend was available.
As it turned out he was actually friends with Joe's oldest
son. In any event, it would be exciting to meet Pellegrino
in person and we hoped that he would show up.

Joe offered to take us for a tour of his yard. We accepted.
His garden was typical Italian in that almost every square
inch was devoted to some fruit or vegetable producing
plant. I was disappointed to find out that the figs were not
in season yet, but he did offer us some fruits from his
kumquat tree. We popped them into our mouths right off
the tree, and they were delicious. Joe had olive trees,
tomatoes, peppers, chickens, a few guard dogs, and much
more on his small plot of land which could not have been

Illustration 25: Gay, Pellegrino, Diego, and Pete

more than a tenth of an acre.

We talked with Joe a little longer and then retired to our
room to begin recording some of our day's adventures.
We were in the middle of collecting our thoughts when our
phone rang. The sound of the phone jolted us back to
reality. Neither of us even knew there was a phone on the
wall. Who could that be? I picked up the phone and

probably said something stupid like, "Hello." I did not think to answer the phone Italian style, "Pronto." There was an unusually long pause before, finally, an Italian male responded from the other end of the line. After a little confusion, I determined that this was Pellegrino Mascolo calling to talk to us.

Illustration 26: Diego and Pellegrino map out their family trees

Now my brain was racing ahead with potential problems. I was excited to meet this potential cousin, but where would we meet? If he wanted to meet us somewhere, would Sophia be able to get us there. I groped for the Italian words to ask him where he was. I found a few appropriate words and to my surprise, he understood me. I discovered that he was at Joe's locked front gate, ten yards away, and needed me to come open it up to let him in.

I raced outside, and, there was Pellegrino with another

friend. I opened the gate and welcomed them into the apartment.

After we finished with introductions we found out that Pellegrino's friend was Diego Sorice, another potential cousin through my maternal grandmother, Adelina Sorice. I think Pellegrino knew of my "Sorice" family connection but I wasn't sure that was the reason he came with Diego. In any event, I got to meet two maybe-related people.

Neither of the boys spoke English, but with the help of the

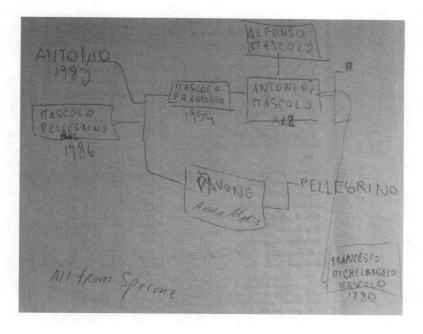

Illustration 27: Famiglia di Pellegrino Mascolo

translation software on Pellegrino's smart phone, we managed to discuss our adventures. We told them all that had happened to us up to this date, and then the subject turned to genealogy. We began to map out their families. We created two family trees; one for Pellegrino and one for Diego. They wrote down all the names and dates that they knew. I made them a promise to look over the data to see if there was a family connection.

Around that time, Joe walked into the room to see how we were getting along and immediately, there was a significant improvement in the level of communications. We talked on into the early hours of the evening. It was already a very satisfying visit for Gay and I, when Pellegrino invited us to his home for dinner. It was about 6:30 at this point. Pellegrino told us that he would go home, and later, at dinner time, he would come to pick us up, perhaps around 8:00 PM.

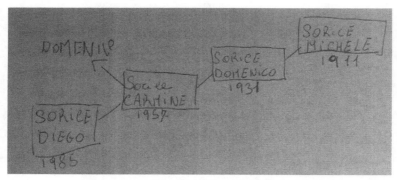

Illustration 28: Famiglia di Diego Sorice

Eight PM! Are you kidding? What happened to the 5:00 PM dinner call? But, after a few seconds of thought, Gay and I decided this might be a really nice thing, so we accepted. With the invitation accepted, we bid Pellegrino and Diego farewell and continued collating our notes of the day.

We wrapped up our note collation around 7:30, and washed up for dinner. We waited for the phone to ring. We were beginning to wonder about the reliability of our evening plan when, around 9:00 PM, we got the call from Pellegrino. He was in front of Joe's house ready to pick us up. We got in the car with him and he drove the few miles to his home in Sperone. There we found a very busy Diego, working on the evening meal. I gathered that Diego had some chef training. I asked if the boys lived there together. Pellegrino explained that this was the home of his parents, but they were out at a festival of some sort. They would be home a little later.

After a while, Pellegrino and Diego brought out what I thought was the entire meal. It appeared to be a plate of

Illustration 29: First of four courses

focaccia bread along with a casserole of potatoes, some prosciutto, cheese, and truffle (mushrooms). We also had an unending supply of homemade wine. This was our first meal in a real Italian home. The food was very good and I was quite satisfied with the food that had been placed on the table when, to my surprise, the boys brought out a second course. This time it is was pasta with tomatoes and more mushrooms, and of course, more wine.

We were beginning this course when Pellegrino's mother and father walked in. They seemed genuinely happy to meet us and they joined us at the table. We had a pleasant conversation with the help of Pellegrino's smart phone. We discovered that Pellegrino is studying to be a medical technician. We discovered that his father, Francesco, was a fruit and vegetable dealer.

Illustration 30: Anna Maria Pavone, Diego Sorice, Pellegrino and Francesco Mascolo

While the conversation was taking place I could see Pellegrino's mother, Anna Maria bustling about the fire in the very handsome fireplace located in the corner of their dining room. What I discovered is that she was busy cooking the steak which was served with a wonderful salad as a third and main course. What a surprise. Now we were in trouble. Our overindulgence of the first two courses forced us to slow down on the "meat" course.

The night went on and we were thoroughly enjoying the camaraderie. We talked about everything from vegetables to politics. I discovered how true the old adage is that the grass always looks greener on the other side. While the family explained to us how difficult things can be in Italy, we explained to them how tragically divided our country has become.

We finished the evening with Anna Maria's Colomba di Pasqua and some coffee (Italian Style). At this point it was near midnight. It was already three hours past our normal bedtime, but we were having such a wonderful time, it did not matter. The Mascolos, however, were facing a work day, so we said our goodbyes and Pellegrino drove us back to Quadrelle to our apartment. It was near 1:00 AM when we finally crawled into our bed.

The Archivio Di Stato in Avellino

It is now Monday, and, according to their website, the Avellino Archivio di Stato is open all day. This was to be our first real test of using Joe's Italian GPS and our first ever visit to an Archivio di Stato. We were looking forward to the planned research of records as well as the visit to a city, Avellino.

We had some pastry and coffee for breakfast and we packed up our electronic devices to begin the day's adventure. On the way out, we met Joe and got some last minute GPS instructions. He was going to also be in Avellino this day, for his work, and he promised to stop by the Archives and check in on us to see if we needed any help.

We got in the car and successfully programmed the address of the Archives into Sophia, and we were off. The roads out in the country were quite reasonable as far as traffic goes. They are, of course, one lane, but we managed to go quick enough so as to not draw too many malocchi.

We got on the AutoStrada for the short ride to the city.

Illustration 31: Streets of Avellino

When we got off the AutoStrada and drew closer to
Avellino, the roads became increasingly congested. While
they weren't the narrowest streets we had seen, they were
quite busy It was obviously rush hour in Avellino.

Things became more and more hectic as we drove down
one congested street after the other. Panic was setting in
because I was not sure how close to the Archive we were.
Sophia started doing some recalculating and then we
decided we were close enough to walk and it was time to
find a place to park.

We made one more turn, and all of a sudden, we were on a
wide extended plaza and there was no traffic to speak of.
Actually, there was no traffic at all. It was like Padre Pio
had heard my prayers and found us a nice peaceful street.
Down the plaza we drove, looking for a place to park.
There was literally no other cars and all we had to contend
with were a few bothersome pedestrians who seemed to be
staring at us and walking nonchalantly down the street as
if they had the right of way and need not be cautious of
moving vehicles.

Suddenly, I remembered something I had read about
"restricted zones" in Italy. I spotted a few polliziotti
ahead, and I had visions of concluding my vacation in an
Italian jail. We turned as quickly as we could before we
reached the policemen, hiding our faces from them as we
went around the corner. We reentered the vehicle
congested streets, and, mercifully, came upon a parking
garage.
After inquiring as to the location of the Archivio di Stato,

we walked calmly back across the pedestrian mall trying to look like ordinary Italians on business.

This particular pedestrian mall was about a half mile long and about one hundred yards wide. It was paved with cobblestones and was lined with numerous shops and restaurants. It was really a nice mall. It was very nice to casually stroll along and not worry about vehicular traffic

Illustration 32: Archivio di Stato - Avellino

(if you know what I mean).

When we reached the Archivio di Stato, we were surprised to find it located about a block off the plaza within a moated palazzo type building. Inside the main entrance wall we found an inner courtyard which was large enough to provide parking for at least 15 or 20 vehicles. There were only two or three vehicles there at the time. The parking here was free and I had no idea how much the parking at the paid lot was going to cost me. Live and learn!

We entered the building, and found a museum quality display of ancient documents in the foyer. Some of them dated as far back as the early 16th century. Perhaps there were older ones as well. We could have spent several hours looking over the displays, but we wanted to begin our research. After all, that is the major reason we came here.

To enter the main library area, we had to state our business and sign in. The librarians were very helpful and we asked if we could see a catalog of their archives so that we could select specific records for research. They were happy to oblige and we selected several years of civil death records. We filled out a formal request, and then one of the officials walked off with an empty book cart.

We sat down to wait. The main research area was like a library room with large tables lined up. The room was about thirty feet wide and 20 feet long. On one side, there was a row of offices for the librarians. Despite the overcast day outside, there was ample light from the large overhead skylights. There were several other researchers there, all staring intently at their work. After some time, the official returned with a cart load of old books, bound up in string. The books were so old that flakes of paper were shedding from them. I'm not sure which looked older, the books or the string.

We carefully removed the strings that were holding the

books together. More flakes of paper fell on the table as we gently opened the books up to view the records. It was a surprise to us that we were not asked to put gloves on.

It was not easy reading many of these records, but we did the best we could and we found several previously known records and discovered two new records. We photographed the pertinent records, and then, as we finished each book, we gently closed them, tied them neatly back together, and returned the old books to the cart.

Illustration 33: One of the more difficult books to read

We spent several hours with the death records, and it was now near lunch time. The food in the vending machine didn't look too appetizing so we decided to find a place to get some lunch and come back to spend the afternoon examining birth records.

The section of Avellino we were in was full of shops, restaurants and small bars. We found a nice place on a corner street and enjoyed some calzones as we watched the business people and shoppers walking by. The bar was spotless and the display cases were loaded with tempting looking food and desserts. We could have stayed here all afternoon just hanging out, but we're here for research and research it will be.

Illustration 34: Lunch in Avellino

So we returned to the Archives and this time, as we entered, we spent a little more time looking at their museum. When we signed back in we had the pleasure of meeting Carlo Guardascione one of the Archive directors. We knew Carlo, at least by name, from some earlier email correspondence. He had responded to one of our requests and actually provided some very useful information.

For our afternoon session, we requested some birth records

and after a while, the attendant came out with another cartload of ancient books. As we began to search through these books, Joe DeSimone showed up and looked over our shoulder for a few moments. He was happy to see that we were doing alright and went to do some research of his own. We found several more records and photographed them.

Sometime around late afternoon, we decided it was time to quit. We paid our photographing fees, a small fee for each digital photo we took. Packing our bags and saying arrivederci, we made our way back to the parking garage.

Illustration 35: The concert pianist

On the trip home, we decided to take an alternate country route and stay off the AutoStrada. We went up and down numerous hills passing one town after another. It was a longer ride, but we got to see more of the small towns and more of the countryside.

When we got back to the house, we heard the quiet strains of classical music floating through the hallway. Joe's son was practicing his piano. He is studying classical piano in school, and he is quite an accomplished pianist. We asked if we could listen and he was glad to consent. It was like a private concert. He enchanted us with several wonderful pieces. We talked for a while, and then we went to our rooms to clean up for dinner.

Just a few blocks away there was a small restaurant that Joe had recommended. We walked the short distance and took a chance on ordering a pizza with a name we could not recognize. It was supposed to be the house specialty and when the waiter brought it out, we found it indeed unique.

Illustration 36: Monday night dinner, Quadrelle Pizza

We had some nice wine to drink and we were enjoying the people in the restaurant. In particular, the function room was alive with music and clowns, celebrating the birthday of a young child.

We enjoyed the pizza despite its odd shape. It was, indeed, the strangest looking pizza we had ever seen. We ate slowly and were entertained by watching the people come and go. Reluctantly we left the cozy atmosphere of the restaurant and walked back to our apartment. It was a cool drizzly evening and, thankfully, we had to walk only a few short blocks. Strangely, the wet weather did not bother us at all. We were living a dream.

When we returned, Joe came in and we settled our room bill. Additionally, we struck a bargain to buy his GPS for the rest of our trip. So, for a hundred euros, I was now the proud owner of Sophia, our Italian speaking GPS.

Tomorrow, her first task would be to get us to the Salerno Archivio di Stato. There, we hoped to meet our friend Maria Fernanda, and present her with a gift in appreciation for the records she had found for us.

We had previously sent several requests to her via email and she found some important records for us. One of her finds was a wedding "allegati" complete with several birth and death records. This was a tremendous find. We were also going to search for other Barbella records from their library of Sassano records.

We concluded the evening with some last minute business

and planning and retired for our final night in Quadrelle.
We were, more or less, pleased with the first three days of
our adventure and eager to proceed to the next phase.
Little did we realize what was about to take place.

The Disaster in Salerno

We woke early the next morning and got ready to get on
the road. I made a little coffee with the percolator in the
kitchen and we ate those extra special pastries that we had
squirreled away from the American Bar. The pastries were
wonderful but they were a scant reward for the absolute
horror that was to follow.

We said farewell to the DeSimones and thanked them for
their hospitality. Piling our things into the FIAT, we
programmed Sophia to direct us to the Archivio di Stato in
Salerno, and we were on our way to the second phase of
our adventure. Our plan was to spend the afternoon at the
Archivio, looking over Barbella records from Sassano. We
would have a meal in Salerno and then begin our trip to
the homeland of Pietro Barbella, Sassano.

Salerno was no more than twenty kilometers from
Quadrelle so we were expecting a fairly quick trip. Sophia
put us on an AutoStrada so it wasn't long before we were
on the outskirts of Salerno. If we were smart, we would
have parked the FIAT on the outskirts somewhere and
found another way to get inside the city. We were not
smart.

There is a point where fearlessness can slowly transform

itself into stupidity and we reached that point as soon as we entered the main part of the city. Driving in Salerno was a nightmare. Almost immediately, we ran into the most intense rush hour traffic on the narrowest streets we have ever encountered in any city. I couldn't have stopped if I wanted to. There was no place to pull over.

With single minded focus on the Archivio di Stato and no focus on sanity, we pressed on. We got into a line of bumper to bumper traffic, with horns blaring all around us. I don't know how many times we were sure we were traveling the wrong way on a one way street with someone behind us, pushing us along. To make matters worse, Sophia was barking turns at a maddening rate and we had no idea how far we were from the Archive.

I pressed on and although Joe had told me that there was a "traffic restricted" area in the center of town, we did not know what symbol would denote that area on a road sign. We wouldn't have seen it if we ran into it, which is what we did.

Sophia was little help. She began recalculating almost every few seconds. I don't think she knew where we were but we were sure her erratic commands were a sign that we were close enough to walk to the Archivio. We began looking for a parking spot. This was a fool's errand. Believe me, you couldn't park a bicycle, sideways, anywhere on the streets we were on. The cars were packed like sardines and every one of them had their rear view mirrors turned in.

We finally reached an area where the cars were not packed like sardines. Yet every where we looked there were signs banning vehicle parking. On instinct, I made a turn towards the direction I thought the Archive was in and we found ourselves in an alley which allowed the FIAT to pass, with, literally, inches on each side.

I drove slowly, nearly knocking over a parked motor scooter. There were stone buildings on either side of the car that went up at least three stories. Gay and I could have knocked on the doors of these buildings on each side of the street as we were creeping by. It was like driving in a narrow tunnel. I made a slight turn around a curve in the alley and to my utter horror encountered a steel post in the middle of the street, blocking any vehicular progress.

What now! Please don't tell me I have to back the FIAT all the way out of this narrow alley. I could almost feel the stone walls egging me on to scratch my pretty FIAT. How were we going to get out of this mess?

I was in a spot where Gay, who was deep into a Stage IV apoplexy, couldn't even open the door enough to step out and help me back out.

I managed to reverse to a spot where she could get out. She looked over the situation and promptly decided that turning the FIAT's rear view mirrors inward was the only way to avoid the walls. That was a big help.

I barked[7] at her to put them back so I could have a chance

---

7   At this point, we were reduced to barking at each other. That was

to see what I was doing. I started creeping backwards, inch by inch, trying my best to control the gas and the clutch to not jerk the vehicle into the stone walls. I was making some progress when a man came along. He was trying to walk down the alley. The car was wedged so tightly that this poor man could not pass and go along his way. I could feel the burning malocchi aimed directly at me.

The man stepped into a doorway and a few minutes later I had inched my way back enough that he could continue on his way. I called out, "Buon giorno!" I hope he didn't miss his appointment.

What was actually about 5 minutes seemed like 5 hours as I inched my way back, little by little to the corner where I had made the disastrous turn that landed me in this alley. I managed to get myself back on the road I had come in on and was about to get out of there, when another car came down the street towards me. This was not a two way street. I had to turn back into the alley to allow him to go by. Then I had to inch myself back out once again. This time, when we got out, we had clear sailing out of the one way street and back into an open piazza.

We found a couple of paper bags to breath into to restore our normal breathing rate, then I stopped someone and inquired about the Archive. I don't know exactly why I cared any more but I did. I was told it was a short distance away but that I was in a restricted area and should exit

---

the only way to relieve some of the pressure which threatened to blow us up into Italian oblivion.

quickly. I kind of knew that.

When I got back into the pandemonium of the city streets, we started looking, to no avail, for a parking space. We would have taken any place we could find. Suddenly there appeared a steep driveway, going down underneath a building, and a nearby sign said "Parking Garage". I must have been so excited to find this sign that I missed another word on it, "Uscita". I started down the narrow ramp only to find the garage attendant running up the ramp flailing his arms furiously at me. This was the exit ramp. Now I not only had to back up a steep narrow ramp, but I also had to back out onto a busy crowded narrow street.

I don't know how I managed to do this, but when I was back on the street I yelled **"ZIO."** For those of you who do not speak Italian, that's **"UNCLE."** That was enough. We drove until we found a fairly wide street that appeared to be leaving Salerno.

Maria Fernando, I apologize. I wanted to thank you, in person, and leave you a gift for the wonderful allegati you had sent me. It will have to wait for another time when I have the good sense to take a train into Salerno.

When the road got wide enough, we pulled over and told Sophia to "take us to Sassano, **NOW!**"

Sassano

After our fiasco on the streets of Salerno, we programmed Sophia to take us to the church of San Rocco in the village of Sassano, our next stop. We were quite happy to escape the city and get back on the AutoStrada but I was a little apprehensive about getting to our next stopping point, the Park Hotel Montpellier.

Illustration 37: The rain was persistent

You see, I had several emails and a few phone calls with the Trotta brothers who run the hotel. I made the reservations through the email and I saw pictures of the hotel on their website. It looked like a very nice place. Yet it contrasted sharply with other pictures we had seen of old Sassano, full of antique buildings.

I asked the Trotta brothers for the hotel address so that I

could enter it into my trip notes. They told me to simply drive to the newly constructed church of San Rocco. The hotel didn't seem to have a valid address. They assured me that I would see the hotel from the church.

Now there are a lot of San Rocco's in Italy, but I managed to find a web site for the church of San Rocco in Sassano. It showed pictures of the newly built church and gave me an address for my address book. However, when I used that address to try to find the church on Google Maps, all I saw was an open field. As far as Google was concerned, there did not appear to be a church, nor did there appear to be a hotel. Apparently, when Google took its pictures, neither the hotel or the church had yet been built.

The result is I had some doubts about the address we had fed to Sophia, and I had some visions of staring at an open field at the moment Sophia announced, "Arriva!" If that happened, I would have to find an alternative place to stay when we got there.

Sophia was, of course, not concerned about any of this, so she took us south for about an hour after which we finally left the AutoStrada. The road became more country like as we drove on our way. The weather was not what you would like, but I was so excited to be going to Sassano that I did not care about the rain that was falling at a fairly heavy rate.

The terrain became more mountainous as we drove further and further south. The clouds hung low over those mountains in front of us as if they were trying to hide the

mountain tops from our eyes. The sky darkened, making
for an ominous scene. We began to see houses closer and
closer to the roadsides until, finally, we felt like we were
intruding, just by riding by. We started to see beautiful
hillside communities with their homes built close together
on the slopes of the many large hills we were driving by.
Invariably, there would be a church steeple near the top of
these hillside towns. Somehow, more and more, I had an

Illustration 38: The perplexing sign - Now What?

intangible feeling that I was coming home.
A few miles away from Sassano, we encountered the
perplexing sign that you see in illustration 38. OK! Now
what do I do? Sophia directed us to the left, and that
turned out to be the correct direction. Soon we rode into
the village of Sassano, another hillside community which I
almost immediately recognized from internet pictures that
I had been studying. We could see the buildings up the
side of the hill. With great relief, we also saw another very

familiar sight, the church of San Rocco. It was exactly as it was pictured on its web site, and now, here it was.

We pulled up into the parking lot of the church and began looking for our hotel, the Park Hotel Montpellier. There it was, about a quarter mile away, as described by its owner in our email exchange. What a sight for sore eyes.

Illustration 39: The Park Hotel Montpellier (alias, the Sassano Taj Mahal)

We recognized the building immediately from the hotel's web site pictures that we had studied before we began our adventure[8]. It is difficult to describe what the hotel looked like. It was obviously a very new structure and it was the dominating feature on a small rise at the foot of the hillside town. It was surrounded by very old Italian homes. It simply looked out of place in time and in space. It was almost as if the hotel building had dropped on Sassano

---

8 Grazie di Dio for the internet

from some futuristic world. It simply looked strange standing there amid all the antiquity, yet, that was not the strangest thing we were about to encounter.

The Park Hotel Montpellier

Off the main highway was a short curved road that wound its way from behind the new church up to the hotel. We drove up this road from the church of San Rocco to the hotel and entered an empty and unpaved parking lot that was on the bottom level of the five story building. We could not drive up the road to the hotel entrance on the second level because a large iron gate was closed, blocking

Illustration 40: Knock Knock, anybody home

our way.

At the lower level, there was a covered parking area underneath the building. We drove up to this parking area and noticed a lot of construction equipment and an old vehicle sitting there rather forlornly. We chose to park the FIAT out in the open dirt parking area.

We stepped out of the car and walked up a long set of stairs to the main entrance area. There was a side door there, but, to our surprise, it was locked. We knocked on this door to no avail. There didn't seem to be anyone on this end of the hotel. Obviously the main entrance was on the other end of the hotel.

On our way to the other side of the hotel, we next walked by the windows of a large function room. Here, we found some promising signs of life. There was confetti all over the floor from some festa that had been recently celebrated there. We knocked on the windows of the function room, but again, there was no one in sight.

We continued walking until we came to what was certainly the main entrance to the hotel. Here we could see the front desk, and although there was no one in sight, we would be sure to find someone here. We stepped confidently up to the automatic door; but, to our complete shock, it did not open. Now, adrenalin was flowing and a little panic was setting in.

We knocked on this door a little louder and a little longer than before. Still there was no answer. We knocked again, even louder and longer. Still no answer. We could see no one at the front desk and we could see no one in the dining hall adjoining the front lobby. Is this possible? Could the main hotel in the town be closed? Did they go out of business? We could see that the driveway coming up from the road to the main level was completely blocked by that large iron gate and there were no other cars around. What a revolting development this was.

We decided to go back to the FIAT and drive down towards the town. Perhaps we could find someone who knew the status of the hotel. Perhaps they could direct us to another place of lodging. We didn't relish the thought of sleeping in the FIAT.

We drove out of the parking lot and turned toward the town. Just a few yards away from the hotel entrance we came to the driveway of a fairly large house and I decided to enter the driveway, look for life and make an inquiry. Maybe the hotel's neighbor would know something of the hotel's status.

A young man walked out as we were approaching the house and I managed to ask him if he knew why the hotel was closed. He looked at the strange Americani quizzically[9], then he turned and looked at the hotel with just a slight expression of exasperation. I wasn't expecting too much from this young man, but to my surprise, he asked me to wait a moment. He took out his cell phone and made a call.

After a few moments on the phone, he clicked it shut and told me that he had talked with the owner and the hotel would be open soon. He apparently knew the Trotta

---

9   Probably thinking to himself, "why are two Americans coming to Sassano in April?"

brothers who ran the hotel and he had called them to wake them from their afternoon siesta. In any event, before we could drive out of the young man's driveway, we could see the iron gate to the hotel opening up automatically. That's more like it.

Illustration 41: Gay befriends our quartz heater

This time, I drove the FIAT up the driveway to the main level and unpacked the bags. We walked up to the door, and to our great relief, it opened automatically for us and we introduced ourselves to "Trotta brother numero uno". Of burly build and with a day's beard growth, Trotta brother I sat, mute, behind the front desk and acted as if nothing unusual had just happened. He made no attempt to apologize for being closed when we arrived. He also showed no signs of annoyance at being woken from his siesta, but, instead, we got down to essential business and made fast work of the sign in procedure. We did not have to stand in line. The sign in was little more than showing our passports. To make copies, Trotta I asked us to leave

our passports with him. We were a little uneasy about
that, but we did, and he then escorted us to our room.

Our room, the marriage suite, no less, was on the 2nd floor
of the hotel. It was very clean and far more comfortable
than I was expecting. From the attached balcony, we had a
magnificent view of the newly built church of San Rocco
down the road. It was still rainy and cool outside, so a
room quartz heater quickly became our friend.

The room was equipped with a king size bed, a flat screen
TV, and a very clean bathroom. The reasonable room rate
also included a breakfast. What, to our total surprise, the
hotel did not have was - other guests.

Illustration 42: View from our balcony

It was hard to believe, but we were the only ones staying at
this large hotel on this cold April day. When I asked why, I
was told that it is off-season. Apparently August is the big

season in Sassano. That's interesting, because I believe it is also brutally hot here in August. Yet, I know that there are numerous and large religious festivals then, so his answer made at least a little sense. Still, I wondered about the overhead of keeping a nearly empty hotel. How were the Trotta brothers financing this place?

It was time for lunch, so we went to the lobby and asked Trotta brother I about places to eat. We were told that La Campagnola was open for lunch and was only a few kilometers away down the main street.

Illustration 43: Domenico, our waiter at La Campagnola

So, with our place of lodging secure, we set out for some Southern Italian nourishment. We found the restaurant with no trouble, down the road by a small stream. We entered to find a dozen or so empty tables inside. The waiter, Domenico, was a personable chap with a decent handle on English. We asked if the restaurant was open.

"Certo, Certo," he said as he handed us menus and recommended the day's special, pasta fagioli. That sounded good to us, so we agreed with his choice and were rewarded with the best pasta fagioli that we had ever tasted. I had a small suspicion that, somehow, the stress of the Salerno disaster and the closed hotel had built up our appetites to the point that anything would taste good, but this was an extremely satisfying meal.

The Mountain Climbers

When we finished our lunch, there wasn't much food left in the bowls. But now it was time to get down to the business of checking out the ancient hillside village of Sassano.

On the computer, we had studied the village of Sassano at length. We watched movies of cars driving up its streets. We knew what the new church, San Rocco, looked like. We knew what the old church at the top of the village, San Giovanni Evangelista, looked like. We had seen many pictures of the village on the hill. Now it was time to go visit some of these places in the home town of my great grandfather and bring the pictures to life.

The road took us towards the old town on the hill and we could see the ancient mother church, near the top of the town. This is the church where parish records were kept. This was the church where my great grandfather, Pietro, was baptized. Our mission was to get to the church, gain admission, and examine old records.
We drove, using instinct, to find our way towards the

church and we found ourselves in a small open area with several roads to take. Unfortunately, they were not wide enough to suit us. Unbelievably, these streets were more narrow than the streets of Salerno. Not only that, but they were steeply inclined upwards at what looked like a thirty degree angle. Gay began hyperventilating so we parked the car and made a command decision to walk.

Illustration 44: Showing the masons how to use the tool

While we had been driving toward the village, we could see the bell tower of the old church in front of us, but from our current location in this mini piazza the steep incline was blocking our view. We could not see the tower, making us uncertain which of the many paths to take. However, we were fairly certain that the church was not too far away.

There were some masons working on the side of a building in the piazza. I decided to ask them for a little help. I approached them and asked if they could direct us to the church of San Giovanni. Even though they looked at us as if we had two heads, they were friendly enough so we engaged them in some polite conversation.

They told us that the church was just a few hundred meters up the street. What they failed to say is that the street was straight up. We talked for a while and I threw some names around. The men new the names of my ancestors, Galatro and Fornino, but they did not know the name Barbella. The genealogical fact is that most of the Sassano Barbellas either died very young, or left the village a very long time ago. A pioneering spirit and the lure of America was in their blood.

We began to walk in the direction the men had suggested to us and, as we suspected, it was indeed, a mountain climb. Narrow cobblestone streets were lined with old houses, all seemingly connected. It's like the village was one big house, all the way up the mountain. There were no lawns or even yards visible anywhere. We passed one shop, a pharmacy, and another shop, a bakery, on our way up the hill. I showed remarkable restraint by not entering the bakery. At this point of the uphill huffing and puffing, a pastry would probably have killed me anyway.

The ascent was difficult and challenging, but it was an exercise made light by the fact that we were here, in Sassano, walking the streets of my Barbella ancestors. We encountered no people until we were very near the top. There, just around the corner from the church, we found two young women sitting on a stoop in the drizzle. We passed them and walked up to the church feeling their stares behind us. We turned the last corner and there, in front of us, was the Chiesa di San Giovanni Evangelista. Here it was! What a thrill to simply be standing here.

As we expected, the door to the church was closed. We walked around the church and found a small piazza, overlooking the village. The view was magnificent. The village lay beneath us, in silence. We looked out and heard no sound other than a few dogs running around the piazza. Patches of blue sky were visible and the red tiled roofs of the homes seemed to go on forever.

Illustration 45: Chiesa di San Giovanni Evangelista, Sassano's mother church

It was early afternoon, and although the view was lovely, it was clear that we were not going to get into the church at this hour. We needed more information about the church. We needed to talk with Don Otello Russo, the local priest, to arrange a time to see the old records. We began to head back down, following our trail of breadcrumbs that we had carefully strewn along the cobblestones through the twisty hilly streets.

We decided to see if we could extract any information from

the two young women sitting on the stoop. We asked if they knew when the church would be open. They said the mass was at 5:30 PM every evening.

Illustration 46: View from the church piazza

We talked a little more with the girls. Anna and her friend were very polite and they listened to our story; why we were here, and what we were looking for. They were fascinated to encounter two crazy Americani in their village. This was a first for them. Clearly they were excited by our presence but we did not know exactly how excited Anna was until a few more days had passed.

We told them we would be back for the mass tomorrow evening and we said goodbye and continued down the mountain hoping to hit the bottom somewhere near where we parked the car.

When we reached the masons I decided to try to have a

little fun with them. In jest, I reprimanded them, huffing and puffing as if I were completely out of breath[10]. "Two hundred meters," I cried out. "It was two kilometers!" I huffed and puffed a little harder. In mock indignation they challenged my assessment of the distance as well as my stamina and we all had a good laugh.

Illustration 47: Firewood in April, really?

We met another man in the street, carrying a wheelbarrow of firewood. He was also interested in the two crazy Americani. At this point, we began to feel eyes from within the homes, staring, in curiosity, at the two strangers stalking about their town. We were becoming local news if not local legends. Word was spreading fast that strangers were on the loose.

We went back to our room in the hotel, and I was ready for a siesta. Not so, the boss! Gay wasn't about to waste good sight seeing time in a siesta. She decided to walk down the

---

10 Which I was!

street to the new church, San Rocco, near the hotel to see what it was like. I stayed in the hotel room for a while, catching up on notes and emails. Then I, too, walked down the road to join her.

Illustration 48: Chiesa di San Rocco, Sassano

Being the newest place of worship in Sassano, the church of San Rocco was unlike any church we had seen so far in Italy. First off, it was a surprise to find it open. It obviously was in violation of the Di Simone rule. The interior was cool and spotless and also, very bright. The altar was brilliantly illuminated with natural sunlight despite the multitudinous clouds overhead. We sat for a few moments in silence, as though we were catching our breaths from an extended period of exercise. We also got in a prayer or two for our loved ones near and far.

We absorbed the silence for a while and then I decided to make some noise in an attempt to get the attention of anyone who might be in the building. If this church were

open, there must be someone here. Perhaps I could get to
meet Don Otello Russo. He was the key to getting access
to any church records. Maybe he was working in a back
room somewhere.

I went to the front of the altar and knocked on the left side
door. There was no answer. There was no sound from
behind the door. I got the same response from the right
side door.

I walked outside to look around. I found a woman outside
who told me that Don Russo lived in the home adjacent to
the church. I went around the church to approach the
house. There were a half dozen Sassanesi children playing
soccer there on the church grounds, but as I turned around
the outside corner of the church, I could see that the garage
was open and there was no car there. That was not a good
sign. Regardless, I continued on and climbed the steps to
the priest's residence and knocked on the door. Again
there was no answer.

After that, I rejoined Gay and we walked back to our room
and decided to head out for dinner. The hotel concierge
(alias Trotta brother I) recommended a pizzeria near the
place we had taken lunch. The name of the place was
Osteria Santa Chiara. We went there only to find out that
it was not open for dinner just yet. We were about an hour
too early.

So we took a ride down the road and found a more
commercial section of the town. There, we spotted a

supermercato[11] and we decided to go in. The store was not unlike a large chain American supermarket, but there were several notable differences. We found aisles of treats, including baked goods, wine, local meats and fishes.

There was an entire aisle, filled with hundreds of varieties of wine. We found a bottle of our favorite Sangiovese for just 2 Euros. On the other side of the store, we found a corkscrew to open the bottle. That was 4 Euros. OK! We showed remarkable restraint staying away from the cannolis and other cream filled pastries which were abundant.

Illustration 49: At the supermercato

We exited the supermercato with our purchases and went back to the restaurant and this time it was ready for business. We enjoyed a very good pizza and we watched an Italian quiz show on the big screen TV. While we were there a few take-out customers came and went, but, once

---

11 Basically, an Italian grocery store

again, we were the only people in the restaurant. It makes one wonder how any business survives here in April.

The chef, a young man, came out to greet us and see if we were enjoying his pizza. He had been alerted by the waitress that two Americani were here, eating his pizza. He wanted to know how it compared to US pizza. I think he, like many young Italians, had dreams of one day coming to America.

By the time we left the restaurant, it was dark. We drove back to the hotel and we had a wonderful nighttime light display of the village along the hillside. The town was lit up by hundreds of lights in a geometrical pattern which mimicked the placement of the homes on the hillside. The lights twinkled like stars in the night all the way up to the church at the top. Like a scene from a fairy tale, it was beautiful to see.

We got to our room and were quickly settled for the night. We put our bottle of Sangiovese out on the balcony to stay cool. The rain was falling at a fairly steady pace. The weight of a very long day pressed down around us and, as if we needed it, the gentle hum of the quartz heater helped us get to sleep even faster.

Off To Padula

We slept well this, our first night in Sassano. The misadventure in Salerno and the mountain climb had sapped a lot of energy from us, so we took the liberty to sleep just a little longer than usual. By this time we were almost, but not completely, adjusted to the six hour time change forced upon us by our Atlantic Ocean crossing.

For this new day, our goal was a trip to the Museo del Cognome, the museum of surnames. This was a genealogical museum run by Michele Cartusciello in the neighboring town of Padula. Who would believe that in this place, one could find a genealogy museum?

We forced ourselves out of bed, freshened up, and then went downstairs to have our breakfast. We entered the large and quite cool dining room. There we sat, all by ourselves. The breakfast was served up by Trotta brother II. It was quite substantial and very good. We had a large carafe of blood orange juice. There was a large bowl of corn flakes and a carafe of fresh milk. There were croissants and Mrs. Trotta II made a very delicious cake. Trotta brother II made us a few cups of coffee (American style) using a very complicated looking and large espresso machine. This machine had many levers and knobs and was spitting out steam from several ports. It reminded me of Ian Fleming's Chitty Chitty Bang Bang. That would be an apt name for this machine.

We did not get eggs, but, what can you expect for 50 Euros a night. We were not hungry when we left the dining room, and now we had met both of the Trotta brothers.

With breakfast finished, we were ready to head out to Padula to find the Museo del Cognome. We collected our notebooks, our camera and the computer, and we headed out to the car. After feeding Sophia the museum's address, we were off to begin our second day in Sassano.

The museum was less than 10 miles away, but the ride was quite an adventure and, to say the least, quite unique. The back country road was different than any road you might encounter in the US. This kind of cultural variety is exactly what we were looking for. It made the ride ever so much more thrilling.

The road was peppered with small farms. The farm

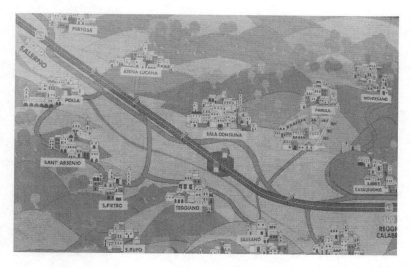

Illustration 50: The hill towns

houses and barns were so close to the road that we could reach out and touch them. Going by them, we had to slow down just to be sure we didn't clip someone coming out of their front door. We encountered sheep, dogs, and other farm animals, and all the time we were praying that no one would be driving in the opposite direction. The road was wide enough for only one car, but, in truth, there were plenty of flat areas that would allow you to move over and let another car by.

After five or six miles of this country road, we turned onto
a larger highway going to Padula. Padula is another one of
the prevalent hill towns in this area. As we approached
the town, we could see the homes, in the distance, spread
across and up the hill. Like Sassano, there was a church
bell tower at the top of the hill.

After driving another mile or so, Sophia commanded us to
go up another very narrow street. Take a look at
illustration 51. This looks like someone's driveway.

Illustration 51: Another Italian 2 way street; really?

Oh Sophia, how could you do this to us. Gay didn't even
bother breathing into the paper bag. She just demanded
that we park and walk. I had no idea how far away the
museum was. I had yet to learn how to read Sophia's face
to find the number which indicated distance-to-

destination. The numbers on the screen were confusing me. I made a decision to try to find a different way up the hill.

There was a small store on the corner of this street. I went in and asked the proprietor if he could tell us how to get to the museum. He told us to drive up the same road that Sophia was telling us to go up. He could not understand why we were hesitant to drive up this side street. I could read his thoughts questioning my manhood, but his actions were to simply shrug his shoulders and tell us it was about 4 km away. That's a little too far to walk. He directed us up another road that was wider and would get us closer.

Illustration 52: Certosa di San Lorenzo, Padula

We drove along a curvy uphill road and came upon a magnificent overlook. There below us was a rich valley countryside and small communities. In the middle of the scene stood the monastery of San Lorenzo. This ancient landmark was on our list of things to see while we were here in Padula.

Also, at this overlook, there was a bronze bust of one Joseph Petrosino. At the time, I did not remember who this was. I simply supposed he was some prominent Padula politician. It didn't dawn on me that there was something extraordinary about giving the statue an American name, Joseph, and not Giuseppe.

Illustration 53: On the road to Padula

We took a few pictures of the magnificent scene before us and got back in the car to continue our search for the museum. The road led us to an open piazza somewhere in the middle of the hillside village. We parked the car and approached some of the locals.

We asked if they knew where the Museo Del Cognome was. We were told it was about a km away, up some narrow street. I went back to the car thinking that, perhaps we ought to skip the museum. There was no way Gay was going to let me drive up those streets. We could walk the distance, but it would take us a while to walk up and back and today, we had limited time. We were deciding on making the hike and consuming the time when we were rescued by another guardian angel. A man approached us and asked, in acceptable English, if we were looking for his friend, Michele Cartusciello and the Museo del Cognome.

I suppose word gets around town quickly when two Americani are wandering about the town looking for something. We said yes, that is where we wanted to walk. He, in turn, began to provide detail directions on how we could get there. Somewhere around the fifth turn he recognized the futility of trying to explain the circuitous route to strangers. He realized the likelihood that we would never find the museum on foot, and he simply asked if we would allow him to drive us there in his car. Are you kidding? What an offer! We all piled into his car.

He proceeded to drive us up unbelievably narrow roadways. With each turn he had us holding our breath as we watched the stone walls of the buildings come within centimeters of his vehicle which was traveling at a speed of at least twenty five miles per hour. As he drove, he recommended that we go see another Padula museum dedicated to Joe Petrosino, a son of Padula. He explained that Joe was a famous New York City policeman who devoted his life to fighting the Mafia. Unfortunately, the Mafia repaid him by gunning him down.

It came to me, then, that Joe Petrosino was also a prominent policeman in the investigation of Maria Barbella, the infamous murderess of 1900 New York City. Maria was known as the first woman to be sentenced to the electric chair in Sing Sing prison. She was found guilty of slitting her lover's throat because he wouldn't marry her. Joe Petrosino was a prominent figure in a book[12] about this murder. I refrained from discussing this with our driver because I was doing everything I could to assure that he concentrated on his driving.

Illustration 54: The Museum of Surnames, Padula

We arrived at the museum in one piece, somehow. The museum was a part of what appeared to be one building covering the entire street. It was as if the street was a long wall designed to ward off invaders. We went into the building and there, we met, for the first time in person, Michele Cartusciello, the genealogist proprietor. We made

---

12 "The Trials of Maria Barbella" by Idanna Pucci 1996

our introductions with the help of our new friend because Michele does not speak a word of English. Despite the language barrier we quickly got down to the business at hand.

Illustration 55: Michele in the middle - our Guardian Angel on the left

Michele showed us his museum and talked about all the work he was doing. In turn we told him about the families we were tracking.

The museum and all its wall displays were interesting and Michele showed us the work he had done to trace American celebrities. They included Frank Sinatra, Dean Martin, and Sylvester Stallone, who happens to come from Palo Del Colle, the next stop on our adventure.

We toured the museum and saw Michele's theater where he teaches genealogy to young people, of all things. I can't imagine trying to do that in the US. Any time I want to get my kids or grandchildren to leave me alone, I simply need to talk about genealogy. They make a beeline for the nearest exit.

We talked about possible research that Michele could do for us in the future. We talked about the records in San Giovanni Evangelista back in Sassano. He did not seem keen on trying to research these, but he suggested that we try to catalog what was available there if we ever got access to them. Rather, he suggested a search of Notary records held at the State Archive in Salerno (You remember, the one we never got to). Michele also suggested that we tour the Sassano Cemetery. He tried to locate it for us on the computer, but he could not.

We exchanged several other pieces of information using Google Translate and then, with our business completed,

Illustration 56: Lunch at the Certosa di San Lorenzo

we got in Michele's car and took another white-knuckle

drive back to our FIAT in the piazza. We said good by and I promised Michele that he would hear from us again. [13]

With an eye on the clock, we drove back down the mountain to the monastery, the Certosa di San Lorenzo. There we parked the car and found a real "touristy" place to have lunch, a little pasta and a little wine. Despite the rampant tourism here, the food was good.

Next we walked down a long road to the monastery entrance and made an abbreviated visit. It is unlikely that we saw all there was to see there at the monastery. It was full of school children, visiting on vacation. The building and its courtyard were impressive but we wanted to make sure that we were back in Sassano for that 5:30 mass at San Giovanni Evangelista up the mountain. It was important for us to make contact with Don Otello Russo if I was ever to get into his office to examine records.

We walked back to the FIAT and began our ride back to Sassano. We were doing well, retracing our route with the help of Sophia when we came upon a shepherd, blocking the road with his flock of woolly sheep. There may have been thirty or forty sheep in the flock. They waddled along the road following their shepherd. Another car pulled behind me, and since the shepherd was now blocking two cars, he went to the right to remove his flock from the road. It did not take him long to clear the road, but it caused us to take a fortuitous wrong turn.

---

13 Indeed he did hear from us again. After our trip we contracted Michele to search out those notary records for us. He did so, and sent us very readable images of four separate documents.

We were on a different road now, not the one we had gone to Padula on, but we could see the old town on the mountain. We could see the church. We knew we were headed in the correct direction. That's when Gay spotted a cimetero, an Italian cemetery.

Illustration 57: Cimetero di Sassano

We had a little time, so we stopped to take a look. The cemetery was open and we walked in. Here, we found rows and rows of crypts, built into a green hillside. Each row was about four or five hundred meters in length. Although we were not sure, at first, that this was the Sassano cemetery, after entering, it became evident. When I began reading the names on the crypts, it was crystal clear.

You see, I have been researching Sassano families for several years now. At my local Family History Center I hold all the LDS records for birth, marriage and death from the commune of Sassano. On a special web page, titled the Sassano Project, I have been indexing the births, deaths and weddings of the people of Sassano. In accomplishing all this work, I have begun to feel like I know all the families in the town.

All of a sudden, family names that I had been recording simply jumped out at me. There were no Barbellas, and I was not surprised by that. But here were the Galatros, the Forninos, the Pellegrinos, the Ciorcioris, the Rubinos, the Feminellas, the Biancomanos and so many other names that I have seen over and over again in my studies.

The crypts along the rows were placed very close together and they seemed to go on, endlessly, down the length of the cemetery. Each crypt obviously held several family members, and each was peppered with photos and engravings of the deceased. The crypts were also covered with flowers of all sorts and votive candles.

We remained there for a while, taking the scene in and recording our visit with photographs. We searched in vain for a Barbella crypt, but I knew that the last Barbella had left Sassano over 100 years ago. There was almost no chance that we would find a Barbella burial sight here.

It was getting near time for us to go to church. We had a "date" with Don Otello Russo at 5:30 at the church up the mountain, so we left the cemetery and drove into town, back to our hotel. On the way, I stopped at the San Rocco church to see if Don Otello Russo was at home. Once again I walked around the church towards his quarters, I encountered the children playing soccer and once again I noticed that the garage was empty. The children were curious now. They wanted to know if I was looking for Don Otello. They told me he was not there. I already knew that.

We regrouped in our hotel room and then we went out to climb the mountain again. For sure we would meet up with the Don at this mass.

Second Mountain Climbing Expedition

We set out to our favorite parking piazza at the bottom of the hill. On our way we passed a traveling salesman with a mobile department store. He was driving a large truck from which hung every type of household and kitchen gadget you could imagine. All I could think of was from my early youth when the town junk man would pass through with his wagon looking to buy, sell or swap just about anything.

We arrived at our familiar piazza, parked the car and stepped out to begin our trek. We began to notice that everywhere we went, eyes were now following us. People looked out their windows or came out to see the stranieri walking their streets. We now felt the gaze of the local people following us wherever we went.

We met an elderly woman near the bottom of the hill. She had come out of her house, presumably to stare at the strange couple.   I began to converse with her and I tried to explain to her why it was that we were here. She was interested in our search for family, and she recognized many of the family names we were researching, but had little to say about it. Like most Sassani, there was little interest in genealogy, or researching dead people. When we asked if we could take her picture, she complained that she wasn't in proper dress, but she allowed us to take the

Illustration 58: Making more friends

picture anyway.

It was getting late, so we refrained from any more socializing and huffed and puffed our way back up the cobblestone streets of the mountain, a little quicker this time. We got to the church about 5:00 PM, about a half hour early. There we found our friend Anna hanging out, but, once again, the church was closed. This was upsetting, but, perhaps we were a little early.

Anna insisted that we go back down the hill a short way to her home. She wanted to show us some Sassano hospitality by serving us some cake and coffee and she also wanted us to meet her father, Francesco. Having a few minutes before the beginning of mass, we agreed. Although I was not fond of undoing any part of the mountain climb we had just performed, we accepted

Illustration 59: Anna and her father in their home

Anna's hospitality and went anyway.

Anna's home was about 100 meters down the hill. To get there, we twisted and turned through several of the steep Sassano streets. When we got there, she opened one of the large vault like doors which face the street in the side of one of those block long buildings that make up the old town. The door led to an interior chamber where there were several more doors opening into individual living quarters for several families. She opened one of these and

we were in her home. Anna was excited to bring
Americani home to meet Dad, who, by the way, knew
some English.

Anna brought out a very nice cake, but we took a rain
check on the Italian coffee. We sat and talked for a while.
Anna's father was retired, but he had spent some time in
the US. He talked about the difficulty of finding jobs in
Italy. This was something you could sense by looking
around the village. It seemed, to us, that there were many
unemployed in the streets, yet those we saw were not
malcontents; neither down or out or terribly unhappy.
Most seemed to be getting by nicely, perhaps with the help
of family or friends.

It was getting close to 5:30 when we bid farewell to Anna's
father and with Anna leading the way, we climbed back up
the hill to the church. Surprise! The church was still not
open. Anna thought this was unusual. I thought this was
a complete catastrophe.

Anna took out her phone and called someone. She then
explained to us that the Mass today had been at 8:30 AM.
There was no Mass this evening. The next Mass would be
tomorrow morning at 8:30 AM.

This was very discouraging news. How would we ever
meet Don Otello and arrange to view his archive of vital
records? While it was still a wonderful feeling simply to
be here and to walk the streets of my ancestors, we could
not help but feel somewhat dejected as we descended the
mountain back to the car. Our chances at seeing the vital

records within the mother church were getting slimmer by the hour.

We drove to the hotel with a sense of more than a little panic. At the hotel we broke out our bottle of Sangiovese and washed it down with cold pizza left over from the night before.

Illustration 60: Unbelievable chocolate gelato

Knowing that we needed to drown our sorrows, the FIAT drove us to a wonderful gelataria in the Silla section of town. Here we found the best chocolate gelato that we have ever had. That went a long way to picking up our sagging hopes, but not nearly as much as what happened next.

Buona Sera Don Otello

As we drove back to town we decided to check out Don Otello's residence, just once more. I parked in the San

Rocco driveway and walked around the church. I was met
by one of the young soccer playing boys who told me the
bad news, that Don Otello was out. Indeed, once again, I
could see that the garage door was open and there was no
car in sight. Hope was all but lost.

Just at that moment, as if in the midst of a miracle, a car
came down the driveway and out stepped a man in a black
robe and collar. The boy exclaimed, "Eccolo" (here he is)!
Don Otello was not at all surprised to see me. You should
know that before we made the trip, I had talked with Don
Otello on the telephone and learned that indeed he did
have an archive of old records. Without such prior
knowledge, we might not have ventured on this trip.

Also, I suspect that our presence in town was now known
by everyone. Don Otello knew immediately who I was
and exactly what I wanted. Regardless, I introduced
myself and expressed my desire to see his archives. He
nodded his head, yes and told me to meet him at the
Chiesa sopra (the church up the mountain) at 9:00 AM the
following morning, after mass. He would show me the
records then.

I was so excited, I literally ran back to the car to tell Gay
the good news. Who knows if we would be able to find
anything in his archive. At least we were going to get a
chance to look. That was enough to satisfy me. Back at the
hotel room, we relished our gelato, our luck, and crashed
for the evening.

Third Time's a Charm

Illustration 61: Meeting new friends prior to the Mass

You can't sleep in when you need to climb a mountain to get to an 8:30 Mass. There was no way we were going to miss this appointment so we rose extra early.

Up, showered and dressed, we were ready for the day before 7:00 AM. With great impatience, we had to wait for the breakfast room to be prepared. I think that the Trotta brothers knew we were in a hurry this day because they opened the dining hall a little early for us. We enjoyed another delicious breakfast. It was similar to the breakfast we had yesterday with the croissants replaced by bread and Nutella. We wolfed down our breakfast, collected our tools and drove the FIAT to our now familiar piazza at the foot of the hill.

Up the mountain we climbed one more time. Past the pharmacy and past the bakery one more time. We encountered no one on the way up the mountain, but when we turned the last corner to the church, we were delighted to see the door open and a few people milling around.

Illustration 62: Chiesa di San Giovanni Evangelista - Sassano

We walked in and there was our friend Anna, waiting for us, with a dozen or so ladies, who were all curious about the crazy Amercani. There were perhaps twenty minutes to mass time so we shared the story of our adventure to Italy with the people. They were all excited to meet us. We took some pictures and then we settled down for Mass.

An elderly man began playing the organ to begin the mass and Don Otello processed out to the altar. The inside of the church was a stark contrast to the outside. In its antiquity, the outside seemed almost shabby. The inside was very different. On the right side of the church there was a special altar set up for Padre Pio, one of my favorite clerics. There were a half dozen side altars to various saints. The main altar reminded me of the Immaculate Conception church back in my home town.

Illustration 63: Grazie de Dio for Don Otello Russo

Don Otello said the Mass, gave a short sermon, and said the final prayers, all by 9:00 AM. At that point, we approached the altar to see if we could catch his eye in the sacristy. I wanted to be sure that Don Otello had not forgotten us. I didn't want him leaving without talking to me. I had no need to worry.

Anna joined us at the altar, and before long, Don Otello came out, greeted us as well. He led us to his office in back of the church. There, behind the Don's desk, was a floor to ceiling bookshelf, containing row after row of ancient looking registers. My jaw dropped and I'm sure I was salivating.

At this point, what I really wanted was for the Don to leave me the keys to the church and go about his business. I would spend the day with the records and then lock up.

That was not going to happen.

In fact, I was barely allowed to touch the books. Don Otello was going to do the looking. He asked me what I would like to look up. I was eminently prepared for this question and I asked him to look up some family births in the 1700s. Find the name Barbella anywhere on a birth certificate.

Don Otello got up on a stool and began rummaging through the books. He selected a volume and put it on his desk and began looking at birth indexes. He went through several indices while I looked over his shoulder. He shook his head, no. We found nothing!

I was disappointed. Out of all these books there had to be a record of the presence of the Barbella family in Sassano. It was easy to see that the Don was skeptical. In his tenure as the parish priest here in Sassano, he was in charge of several different parishes and he likely has never encountered the name Barbella anywhere at anytime. The last of us had abandoned the town a very long time ago.

The Don continued to pull books, one after the other, from the shelves. Although I was feeding him likely years for which to search, my knowledge of the correct years was less than 100% certain. I was giving him best guesses. For over an hour we struck out. We persisted and finally, we hit pay dirt.

Thanks to my friend, Maria Fernanda, at the Salerno Archivio di Stato, I had a death record for Vincenzo Barbella. Vincenzo's parents were Michele Barbella and Vittoria di Bella. Their marriage would have occurred somewhere in the mid 18th century.

I asked the Don if he might be able to locate this marriage record. Clearly showing signs of weariness, he went back up on the stool, Don Otello selected another volume and put it on his desk. He began searching, and suddenly he muttered as his finger froze on the page. His eyes lit up. He pointed at the book, and there, in front of me, was a 1734 document, partially in Latin; the marriage of Michele and Vittoria.

Illustration 64: 1734 Marriage Record

The document not only records the marriage date, but also records the parents of the groom and the parents of the bride. This incredible discovery gave me another generation in my family tree, pushing me back, with all probability, to the late 17th century. I was, to say the least, ecstatic, and it showed. My enthusiasm seemed to be catching. Everyone there shared in my delight; Anna, Gay, the organ player, Don Otello, and of course, me. I'm surprised we didn't break out in applause.

We took several photos of this document. We were so relieved to have made this discovery. But it had taken a good portion of time, and we knew that the Don had other tasks to tend to. We thanked him and all the people who were there with us. We left a small donation for the church and we bid farewell.

The walk down the mountain was a lot easier than previous descents, despite a persistent and fairly heavy rainfall. This one document had made the entire trip worthwhile. We were beaming as we drove, soaking wet, back to our hotel room to organize notes, warm up, and dry out.

It was now late morning and we had some time to do a little more research or sightseeing before lunch. We were thinking about the Anagrafe Office or the local library. We weren't sure either would be open at this time. May 1 is Labor Day in Italy.

On the off chance they might be open, we drove to the village hall, and as expected, the office was closed due to the holiday being celebrated.

I noticed a poliziotto standing there, manning the town hall, and I walked over to chat with him. He was the only one on duty today. He was very friendly and quite interested in the two crazy Americani looking for records. He gifted us with several brochures about the town and a very useful map. But, before he allowed me to take a photograph, he had to run inside to get his cap.

Illustration 65: A lone policeman at the town house

The noon hour was approaching, so it was off to La Campagnola for some pasta and wine. This time we had a wonderful lasagna. Once again, we had a very good meal at a very reasonable price. The food and drink were extra pleasurable today, I'm sure, because of our incredible genealogical good fortune. We had much to celebrate.

As we drove away from the restaurant, we received a message from one of our face book friends, Veronica Barbella.

Illustration 66: The celebratory lasagna

Veronica is the daughter of one of my Facebook cugini, Oreste Barbella. I call him a cousin, and with a name as uncommon as "Barbella" we must indeed be related at some level. However, I have traced his family as far back as I can with LDS records, and there is no connection back to the earliest years I have on tape, 1866. One of the problems is that Oreste hails from the village of Montesano sulla Marcelena, some ten kilometers south of Sassano. Unlike Sassano, which is now bereft of Barbellas, there are several Barbella families remaining in Montesano.

In any event, Veronica speaks a little English so she has been serving as our go between. I suggested that we meet for a cup of coffee, somewhere, and Oreste agreed.

Oreste selected a bar somewhere between Sassano and Montesano on the outskirts of Padula. We agreed to meet there for a visit. This was a good thing. Although we wanted to tour more of Sassano, it was our wish to meet as many local people as we could. It would be our privilege

Illustration 67: Giovanna, Veronica, Oreste, and Aurora Barbella

to drive to Padula and meet them.

With little trouble, Sophia brought us to the appointed bar. Oreste brought his wife and two daughters. His son, Antonio, was away at school. Despite the terrible taste of the espresso, we had a wonderful visit.

We learned that Oreste has a "state" job as a restaurant inspector. His oldest daughter, Veronica is attending university in Rome and young Aurora is a middle school student. We talked about their home town. We talked about our home town. Between Veronica's limited English and my limited Italian, we managed to communicate together quite nicely.

Oreste brought the espressos and when I tried to drink mine straight, he stopped me, cautioning that it was very strong. He wanted to make sure I put some milk in it. What he didn't understand is that I already knew it was very strong, and I was simply trying to drink it as fast as I could to get it over with.

We finished our conversation as evening was setting in so we said our farewells and departed. It was really nice to see, in person, people that we have communicated with on social networks. We went back to the hotel, satisfied with our afternoon.

Our plan for this evening was to dine with the Trotta Brothers, but when we sat down in the dining room it was not only empty, it was also uncomfortably cold. So instead we decided to go back to the pizzeria, Osteria Santa Chiara.

This time we had pizza featuring cheese, sausage and corn. We watched a little soccer on the TV, and I found it easy to see how much more exciting this sport seems to be here in Italy. The pizza was wonderful, and I'm not sure why, but there were no leftovers when we left the restaurant.

We slept well in anticipation of our trip, the next day, to Palo del Colle. We were about to drive clear across the country to the Adriatic Sea.

Arrivederci, Sassano

Yesterday was a grand day. We accomplished many things and we deserved a sleep-in day. We got it.

It was late morning by the time we rose and cleaned up and had another wonderful hotel breakfast. Trotta II was there to make our coffee and this time, to our surprise, there was another patron. We did not get to speak with him nor find out why he was in Sassano. Just knowing there was someone else at the hotel made it seem a little more comfortable in some indeterminate way. Sassano is not a place of fabulous wealth. It was good to see even a little more money contributing to its GDP.

Today is Friday. It was important for us to get across the country to Palo del Colle. The Anagrafe office in Palo del Colle was one of our trip objectives and it would be open today, but not for the next two days. Saturday and Sunday were going to be sightseeing days with, perhaps, no genealogical goals.

But first, we agreed that we needed a better photo of the beautiful Sassano cemetery. So after breakfast, we packed up our bags and loaded the FIAT for our imminent long drive across the country. We were (surprise!) first in line at the checkout counter. Our bill was 150 Euros. This was a better bargain than Avellino.

We drove back out to the cemetery. The cemetery was open and we encountered a caretaker. We inquired about a "Barbella" crypt, but, as expected he was not familiar with that name. When we asked him if there was a list of who was buried here, he said no, he did not keep one, but I

Illustration 68: Typical family grave site - Sassano

might find one at the town house.

It was already beyond time for us to leave for Palo, but we both decided that the town house was on the way out of town and would only take a few minutes. So we made one more stop at the Sassano City Hall. It, too, would be open today.

We entered the town house. Unlike our last visit here, the building was bustling with business. Upon inquiry, we determined that if there was a listing for the cemetery, it would be in the Anagrafe office. Now we were faced with a new dilemma. We could not enter the Anagrafe office only to see a cemetery listing. How could we go in there and not ask to see old vital records? So our trip to Palo was going to be delayed just a little bit more.

It was surprising to find only a short line in the office. The official told us there was no cemetery listing but that he would be happy to pull old civil records for us.

He left us, momentarily, to climb up the building stairway and came back with several old books. We scanned them together. I wanted to show him proof that Barbellas really did live in Sassano, so I opened the book to the date that I knew my great grandfather Pietro was born. Sure enough, there he was. To my surprise, the official wasn't very familiar with these records and I had to point out several things to him. This was, possibly, the first time he had ever looked at these old records. He seemed fascinated by my familiarity with the documents.

Illustration 69: Ufficio di Anagrafe - Sassano

He left me there with the records and I found several other interesting things. They allowed me to photograph my finds and they would not accept a payment. I have to say that this type of friendliness and willingness to please really touched me. It left me with a feeling that I was home, more so than I have experienced in a very long time.

All of this research took some time. Now we were in double trouble with our schedule. It was near lunch time, so once again we called on our friends at La Campagnola. This time we had pasta with mussels, and just a little wine. Again, we walked out with our hunger satisfied, and our wallets just a tiny bit lighter.

It was early afternoon. Finally, it's time for Sophia to take us to Palo del Colle; and Gay can't wait to see the land of her grandparents. For that matter, we're both looking forward to another new adventure.

Palo del Colle

Across the Country One and a Half Times

It was extremely difficult to say goodbye to Sassano. We hung around far longer than we should have. I just couldn't pull myself away from the land of my great grandfather. We knew that we had just "scratched the surface" of this community with our short three day visit. But, a plan is a plan so we must go on with it. Besides, having places yet to visit and sights yet to see could be a powerful motivating factor for a return visit.

Our next stop was the hometown of Gay's grandparents, Palo del Colle, a small village near the city of Bari. I suspect that if Gay knew the original plan was to leave Sassano early in order to get some time in the Palo del Colle Anagrafe office, she would have spurred me on a little more. Heck, we would have been out of town after breakfast. However, in a fit of selfishness, I simply did not want to let go of Sassano. We wound up leaving very late.

If we had any chance of making it to the Palo del Colle Anagrafe office, we had to get there quickly, but that was not to be. Somehow, Sophia got herself programmed into a mode which avoids toll roads. As a result we were driving down some very narrow roads through some fairly busy towns. Gay started clutching her hyperventilation paper bag.

When we reached the village of Potenza, almost half way

across the country, we realized the mistake. We were driving through crowded central sections of different villages and the streets were getting narrower and narrower. We decided to reprogram Sophia for toll roads. We still had some euros in our pockets, so the highway tolls weren't going to break us. Unfortunately, recalculation to get us back onto a toll road resulted in a lot of back tracking. Before we realized what was going on, Sophia brought us all the way back west to the outskirts of Salerno.

So we drove and we drove and we drove. The scenery was wonderful and we went through some spectacular countryside. One of the surprises was all the hills that began popping up in the middle of the country. The many hills we passed were dotted with wind turbines along the way, one after the other.

The AutoStrada, while not busy, was certainly full of drivers who go much faster than we were going. After what seemed like a whole day of non-stop driving, we approached the village of Palo del Colle. It was now nearly 6:00 pm. The sun was still high so there was plenty of light, but we had a new problem to contend with.

We were confronted with the day's second GPS challenge. It seems that Sophia accepted the village of Palo del Colle, but did not recognize the street address of Masseria Vero, the farm (agriturismo) where we had reservations. OK, I thought; no problem. I'll just stop in the village and ask for directions. Sooner or later I'm bound to find someone who knows where Masseria Vero is.

So that is what I did. At the first gas station I could find, I
stepped out of the FIAT. I spotted a man there, filling up
his car, and I approached him. I'm not sure why I
bothered, other than he was the only one I could see there.
My initial assessment of this fellow was that his IQ might
not be in double figures.[14] My intuition told me that if my
GPS didn't know where Masseria Vero was, this man
wouldn't know either, but I tried anyway.

Hoping that he would understand my Rosetta Stone
dialect, I asked, "Scusami, conosci Masseria Vero?" While
the man gave me a strange look, to my utter surprise he
told me, "Si." He did know. However, the man's pained
expression and his words led me to understand that there
were many turns along the way and it would be very
difficult to explain.

After some discussion in which hand gestures played a
central role, I succeeded in getting him to tell me the first
steps to getting there by pointing me in the right direction.
I took off down the road and made the left turn that he had
advised, all the time hoping that I was getting a little closer
to Masseria Vero. It wouldn't matter how many times I
had to stop as long as I could record progress by getting
closer each stop. Logic dictates that this philosophy would
get me there sooner or later.

After the turn, we drove about a kilometer and then were
confronted with another intersection. In front of me was

---

14 That's a major fault of mine; that is, making quick assessments of
   people. I'm almost always wrong. For all I knew, this fellow could
   have been Albert Einstein.

some type of apartment complex. To my right there was an open field which appeared abandoned; a dumping ground to used bricks and other refuse. To my left, there was a very nice residential section. The two sides of the road contradicted each other. I had to decide whether to go right or left. At first, we didn't see anyone to ask for help.

Then we spotted a woman walking her small dog. I asked her the same question I had asked the man at the gas station. Once again, to my surprise, I got the same answer. This woman also knew where Masseria Vero was. She began giving me one direction after another. "Go down this street, then turn left. Make the next right and at the fork go left on the dirt road............. ad infinitum", all in Italian.

I think she sensed we were having some difficulty remembering all the steps she was giving us. She rattled off more directions and my eyes grew larger, dimmer, and glazed over until finally, she realized the futility of the task and simply said, "Aspetti." She picked up her dog, got into a nearby car and motioned us to follow her.

After a grueling drive, making a number of turns, she pointed down a long dirt road and indicated we would find Masseria Vero there. We thanked her profusely and began to drive down the road but, in just a short distance, came to another intersection; this time, a three way intersection. We were astonished that there was not a single sign directing us to the farm, but that, indeed, was the case.

There was a man coming down one of the three forks on a cart. I rolled down the FIAT window and asked him if he knew the way to Masseria Vero, and this time, the man shook his head, no. Oh boy! Now what do I do? There is no one else to quiz at this desolate and dusty intersection. I decided we would simply have to try all three roads, one at a time.

I was contemplating which of the three directions I should try first. Knowing how bad my luck is with multiple choice questions, I chose the one that I thought would be least likely to go to the farm. I began to turn down this road when, out of nowhere, a car loomed from behind us and careened straight through the intersection in a cloud of dust and a cacophony of horn honking.

It was the woman with her small dog. As she flew by, she motioned us to follow her. Somehow she had sensed that the two clueless Americani were going to need more help. After a mile or so of dirt road and at least one more (unsigned) turn, she proceeded to drive us right up to the gate of Masseria Vero. We thanked this woman a thousand times over and we even tried to offer her some money for her troubles. She was indignant and refused to take anything. What an angel[15].

So, now here we are, at Masseria Vero. If ever you could imagine a "middle of nowhere", this was it. Looking at the scene, Masseria Vero appeared to be the only building on

---

15 You might, by now, be sensing the recurrent theme of guardian angels that helped us along our way. There are many more to come.

the planet. I don't think that in a thousand years I would
have been able to find this place on my own out here in the
country, especially now that the twilight condition of semi
darkness was upon us.

Illustration 70: Masseria Vero, Palo del Colle

There must be a law against putting up signs in Palo del
Colle. This was worse than the Hertz rental counter at the
airport. I fretted that if Sophia didn't know the roads in
this area and couldn't get me into Masseria Vero, how was
I ever going to get out of here? Could this accommodation
possibly be worth the trouble we would have getting in
and out? But, as you shall see, Masseria Vero was a very
good find, a "jewel" of the trip. It was well worth the long
and confusing journey. On top of that, thanks to more
angels in our future, we never had to worry about
directions for the duration of our stay.

It was evening by the time we got to the farm so there was
no chance of getting back into the village to the Anagrafe

office. This was not a major setback for us. Being the
weekend, the plan for our three days in Palo del Colle was
mostly sightseeing. We had a number of Facebook friends
in this area. Several of them were from the nearby village
of Altamura which was a short distance from Mattera.
These were two places we had planned to visit.[16]

We pulled the FIAT into the ample driveway. After so
many hours sitting in the car, it took a little coaxing to
unwind our bodies and climb out. After a little leg
stretching, we went up the stairs which were the main
entrance to the farm and introduced ourselves to the
young woman who was manning the front desk. Slinging
a newborn baby on one hip, she deftly signed us in with
one hand. She already knew who we were. While she was
expecting two sets of visitors this evening, only we were
American and I guess that our Rosetta Stone dialect gave
us away again.

She explained that her mother-in-law, Maria Vero, would
be along soon. We were looking forward to meeting
Maria. We knew Maria spoke very understandable
English.

A year ago, we had talked with Maria on the telephone
about her agriturismo Bed and Breakfast. We mentioned
that we would be coming for a visit sometime in the near
future. That visit never materialized, but here, a full year
later, we had called and finally made the reservation.
Maria surprised us by remembering our last call. In a mild
reprimand, she wanted to know why we didn't come last

---

16 But, sadly, never got to!

year. Now we were anxious to meet this obviously observant lady in person. While we were waiting, we unpacked the FIAT and moved into our clean and comfortable room.

Illustration 71: Our cozy room at the farm

After settling in, we ventured out to the hall, and there, for the first time, we met Maria Vero. She was unmistakable. She looked exactly like she sounded on the phone. Maria was a pleasant looking Italian grandmotherly type with a very inviting face. Her smile was infectious and her voice was soothing as it uttered English words with an unmistakable Italian accent. She apologized for not being in when we had first arrived. She was at a medical facility with her husband Domenic who was having some knee surgery. Marie was happy to see that we had made it to the farm, and we chatted for some time about our adventures to date.

Illustration 72: Masseria Vero dining area

Maria asked if we were hungry[17] and showed us the way to the dining room. The dining room was located in the basement of the farm. To get there, we had to go outside and down the main stairs to the front patio, then over to another set of stairs to the farm basement. The dining area was softly lit and comfortably cool, thanks to the tile floors and stone walls. It was divided into two distinct rooms. The back room was off the main kitchen, more brightly lit, and held four large tables. The front room was closer to the entrance, much more romantically lit, and held just a few tables. The rooms were tastefully appointed with period pieces, simple furniture, numerous large gourds of all shapes and tables covered by red, white and green tablecloths.

At the time, we were the only patrons and we seated ourselves at one of the tables close to the warmth of the

---

17 Very silly question!

kitchen. Maria began to bring out food; green olives, a
little antipasto and some insalata. By the time we had
sampled her first offering, the next course was on the table.
This included home made bread, cheeses, and, of course,
some very very nice grape juice. Our biggest problem was
figuring out what to try next.

Illustration 73: The farm feast

Before we could decide, Maria brought out some pasta
and meat. We spent a good long time at the table savoring
the delicious food and having a wonderful conversation.
Maria spent some time living in the States. Now she runs
her farm with her family and several farmhands. She
boasted that all the food we were eating was produced
right there on the farm.

We were quite full by the time we quit eating and drinking.
We sat there going over our plans for the next two days,
Saturday and Sunday. There would be little, or no

opportunity for genealogical research at government offices, which, of course, would be closed. But there were several intriguing options available to us.

Illustration 74: Gay getting a lesson in Italian cooking

One of our options was a visit to the city of Altamura, just southeast of Palo del Colle. There we could see the ancient megalithic and mortar less walls used to defend the city. We could also visit their 13th century cathedral.

Just a little further is the ancient city of Matera. There we could visit the ancient "Sassi di Matera", cliff houses dug right into the very rock of the city's river ravine.

We decided to make a final decision in the morning, and went to bed not realizing that any plans we slept on this night were not going to happen. Some very nice people were going to come and provide us with all the entertainment we could handle; good company, good history, and private guided tours of many very interesting local sites.

Vito Tricarico and the Festa della Croce

Illustration 75: How could you hate this face?

We were both exhausted and we were both sleeping extra soundly. Just about the time we entered the deepest part of our sleep we were startled from our slumber by the raucous braying of a donkey. Are you kidding me? I believe the donkey woke up the rooster who started crowing, in turn waking up the geese who started honking, all at an ungodly hour. I began searching for someone to kill for this outrageous affront to our peace and sanity when I remembered, "You're on a farm, stupid. What do you expect." Sleep is overrated anyway. Just make believe the animals are singing Copland's Appalachian Spring to you.

We lay in bed a little longer than usual having a good laugh to ourselves. Finally, we got ourselves up, washed and ready for a day of sightseeing.

We took a short walk outside to see the source of all the morning noise, and then went down to the dining hall and found Marie there, waiting for us. She asked what we would like for breakfast. We were kind of tired of the "continental" bun and Italian coffee so I said, "I wonder if you could make us some scrambled eggs". "Sure", said Marie as she walked outside to the chicken coup to gather a few eggs. Can you beat that?

She then served up perfectly scrambled eggs with some toast, a few croissants, a little fruit, some blood orange juice, a little cheese and a little prosciutto. What a scrumptious breakfast.

I was thinking about just hanging out at the eating table all day when Marie sat down with us to relay a message. She told us that our Facebook friend Vito Tricarico[18] had called the farm earlier to see if we were there. She thought he might want to meet us but she could not say how or where or when. We considered the message nothing more than a curious but meaningless inquiry from which little or nothing would come. Boy! Were we wrong about that.

---

18 Vito Tricarico is a resident of Palo del Colle whom we discovered on social media. We had numerous communications with him. We were fairly certain that there is no direct relation between he and Gay, but he was very friendly to us and he knew we were making this voyage and would be coming to Palo del Colle.

After we finished our meal, we went back to our rooms for some final cleanup before venturing out in the FIAT for who-knows-what sight seeing adventure.

When we were ready to go, we stopped to chat in the lobby with Marie, telling her our plans and looking for her assistance, when, with umbrella in hand, in walks none other than Signor Vito Tricarico.

We recognized Vito immediately from our Facebook pictures. He had a huge smile on his face as he, in turn, recognized us. He introduced himself to us and began speaking rapid fire Italian. Rosetta Stone had not prepared me for this. I asked him as politely as I knew how to slow down, but he seemed very excited to meet us and I was only able to get a few words, here and there.

Marie came to our rescue and we learned that this was a special day in Palo del Colle. On this day there was a religious festival in town and Vito wanted to take us into the village, bring us to the festival

Illustration 76: Signor Vito Tricarico, di Palo del Colle

and, generally, show us some local sights. We thought about this invitation for no more than one or two seconds because it didn't take us long to conclude that Vito was someone we wanted to be with. Just looking at the enthusiasm in Vito's smile assured us that the proposed visit with Vito was going to be far more interesting than cruising the countryside on our own. We couldn't have been more right.

Vito motioned us to come with him, in his car, so, together we climbed into his car and we were off. It wasn't a long drive to get into the village of Palo del Colle, but there are not enough bread crumbs in the world to mark the turns that Vito made on his way out of the countryside and into the town. We were more than happy that Vito was doing the driving.

Illustration 77: 2 way street, Palo del Colle style

Soon after we left the dirt roads of the countryside, we encountered the narrow streets of the village. Vito drove nonchalantly along the labyrinthine streets, as carefree as can be, as Gay was having another fit of claustrophobic apoplexy in the back seat. I wondered what this place must look like at rush hour.

Illustration 78: A parade float for the festa

We passed through a small piazza containing a crowd of people working to put the finishing touches on a dozen or so parade floats. Everywhere we looked there was excited anticipation and electricity in the air . Horses were ready to go. A large cross was mounted on a wagon ready to hitch to a horse. The sacred heart was mounted on another wagon, hitched to two massive oxen who were ready to proceed. Members of the band were congregating and warming up their instruments. The parade was forming. Vito explained that the local clergy were going to lead all the people into the countryside to hold an open air mass.

We drove on a little further and down a few more side streets until Vito found what had to be the only open parking space in the entire town. I was quite impressed with his ability to zero in on this spot on such a crowded street until I discovered it happened to be his spot in front of his own house. That took a little luster off his achievement. We piled out of the car and went inside to meet Vito's wife, Maria.

Maria opened the door with an enthusiastic "bienvenuto". Between Vito and Maria, I'm not sure who had the biggest welcoming smile, nor who was happiest to greet two strange Americani in their home and village. The Tricarico home was beautiful and spotlessly clean both outside and in. There was a large open living area and a large open Kitchen/dining area. In between there was a spiral staircase to the bedrooms above. Just off the stairway there was a very spacious bathroom.

Illustration 79: Three Tricaricos and one Barbella

Both Vito and Maria were about as gracious as two people could possibly be. I think that, simultaneously, Gay and I decided that we had made the right decision to go with the Italian stranger with the common name. Any reservations that we held about dropping our prior plans were completely dissipated. This was like finding gold.

Vito was anxious to take us into the village, on foot, to see the town and some of the goings on at the piazza. We were also anxious, to see the village, so after a brief trip to il bagno, we set out on our first pure sight seeing tour; Palo del Colle.

Illustration 80: These magnificent beasts will carry the cross to the open mass

We walked a short distance down a few narrow streets and then we entered a large and obviously very old piazza where all the pre-festa action seemed to be taking place. The piazza was a large square, paved with tile like stone. It was surrounded by very old stone structures. It's antiquity seemed to radiate out to us from every one of the surrounding walls.

Vito is quite an extraordinary Italian. In his retirement,

Vito has authored and published a book titled, "Erculea Proles", a romance novel rich in the history of the 14th century defense of the country against foreign invasion. The book is packed with history, so we couldn't have selected a better person to guide us about this history rich community.

Vito is also an accomplished poet. His book of poems, "Cavalieri E Vergini Guerriere", is also rich in history.

Illustration 81: Gay and Vito heading for the entrance of the old palace

Vito walked us over to a doorway which turned out to be the entrance to the ancient palace at Palo. He was speaking rapid fire telling us stories about the rulers who long ago owned and maintained this palace. He pointed out which parts of the building were original and which parts had been reconstructed. Vito was talking so fast that I concluded he was afraid he would not have enough time to tell us everything. No amount of pleading could get him to slow down. We think he was simply too excited to have found someone interested in his knowledge of history.

I hated stopping him, but occasionally I had to. I needed to, periodically, take a few moments in order to digest what I was hearing and to translate to Gay what little I was catching of the story. The difficulty we had trying to understand what Vito was telling us was more than made up for simply by the sense of being here in this magnificent place, at this time, with such a wonderful historian.

Illustration 82: Vito and Gay within the walls of the palace

Vito next encountered an old friend standing in the square watching the activity. He introduced us to the man and told him that we were here to see the land of Gay's Tricarico and Lattanzio ancestors. We were also looking for relatives and records. His friend, Giacomo Mittaritona, is a retired contractor who used to have a business with many employees. He was well known in town.

Illustration 83: Vito and Gay discussing Lattanzios with Vito's friend, Giacomo

Giacomo told us that he knew the Lattanzio family. He promised to call them to let them know that we were in town asking about family histories. At the time, we didn't think much would come of this. As it turns out we were terribly underestimating the "word" and resolve of our new Italian friends.

Illustration 84: Church of Santa Maria La Porta

Vito next took us to see a very old and famous local church, la chiesa di Santa Maria La Porta. He was very keen on showing us the dominating feature of the front entrance. This was a circular window enclosed by several sculptures. One of those sculptures depicted Hercules holding up the world (a large circular window) on top of a monster's head. Vito was quick to point out that these were original sculptures. His lively and informative discussion added a whole new dimension to the sights we were absorbing. Instead of just looking at the forest, Vito was helping us to see the trees.

Illustration 85: Gay giving a speech from the Lattanzi balcony

We walked about the town a little more and then we came upon Vito's son Domenico. Now it turns out that Domenico Tricarico was also delighted to meet two Americani. He was also very knowledgeable about the history of the area. Domenico had the added advantage of knowing some English. He was anxious to practice it on us. Vito excused himself to return home to make final preparations for the Festa and Domenico, with great relish, took over the duties of showing us around.

Illustration 86: Narrow passageway into the Palazzo

Domenico already knew of our interest in the Lattanzio family. He brought us down a narrow street and showed us a building which had been owned and used by the Lattanzi[19] family many years ago. The Lattanzi family was a political powerhouse in Palo del Colle in the late 19th and early 20th centuries. Their building was the focal point for many political gatherings. Many a political speech had been delivered from the building's balcony. Gay got into the spirit of the moment by getting up on the balcony and giving a stirring speech, imploring all the Italian Laborers to vote for her party.

---

19 The reader will note the use of the name Lattanzi interchangeably with the name Lattanzio. They should be read as one and the same. All the Lattanzi family in Palo del Colle are descendants of one man, Michele Lattanzi. Somewhere, along the line, an "o" was added to the name, like so many other Italian name changes.

Domenico then showed us another of the many palace buildings in the town. This one had an incredibly narrow entrance way. There was barely room enough for me to walk through it. He explained that this type of entrance made it easy for the local people to defend against invaders. Attackers had to charge down this narrow walkway single file. Inside the main court, defenders met the attackers one at a time coming through the passageway. In this way, a few defenders could thwart numerous attackers.

Domenico's description of this tactical technique was quite a revelation, given that, today, we are more accustomed to military strategies which involve "shock and awe" How many of us have put any thought into the defensive strategies of the 17th century Italians against Muslim invaders. Was this too much information for us; not at all; we were loving it. Without even realizing it, we were getting a wonderful lesson in Italian history.

After some more touring in the old town, Domenico, coordinating by phone with his father, finally brought us back to the family house. It was time to go to the Festa in the countryside. By this time the procession had already reached the carnival area and the open air mass was in progress. We needed to hurry if we were going to get to the mass. We went in two cars; Vito, his wife Marie, his oldest daughter Anna, his son Domenico, Gay and I.

On to The Festa Della Croce

Illustration 87: Departing for the Festa Della Croce

We drove through the village and into the country. We had to weave through a number of horsemen, on their way to the Festa. When we got to the site, there were hundreds of cars lining the street. Somehow, Vito found a place to park just a few yards from the field where the mass was in progress. We got out of the car, anxious to attend our first Festa. This was going to be enjoyable.

We entered the field and saw a throng of people surrounding the makeshift altar. There were hundreds of people there celebrating mass in the center of the open field. The altar was on one end of the field. The people attending the mass were stretched out, like sardines, over an area about the size of a football field. The outer perimeter of this area was surrounded by carnival type attractions and rides. There were numerous food vendors and carnival type games. However, for the most part, the hoard of people was focused not on the food and games, but rather on the mass. Their eyes were riveted on the actions of the priest. Their ears were tuned in to his words.

Illustration 88: At the Festa Della Croce

After Mass, we walked about the grounds for a few minutes, sampling a little of the food, and taking in the sights of people enjoying themselves. Was this the "Super Bowl" of festas? Probably not; but it is remarkable how much pleasure the Italian people extract from a simple celebration just like this. The number of cultural differences we were beginning to notice were mounting rapidly. We took delight at being a part of this festa and seeing this side of Italian life.

We stayed for a while, basically people-watching, after which Vito and Marie suggested that it was time to return home. Marie's youngest daughter, Grazia, was home preparing a meal for us. So we climbed back into the car and drove the few miles back to Vito's house.

Illustration 89: At the home of Vito Tricarico

Domenico was already there when we arrived. He introduced us to his girlfriend, and his sister, Grazia. Unlike Vito and Marie, the younger people were anxious to hear spoken English. In contrast, I wanted to hear spoken (slowly) Italian. It made for an interesting mix.

The food was ready, so we sat about the table and feasted on another four course meal. We enjoyed the limited conversation helped by the younger generation's knowledge of English. We talked about family and life in Italy. Grazia expressed her wish to, some day, come to America.

I couldn't help but think how the grass always seems greener on the other side of the street. This is not the Italy of 1875 that forced thousands to flee poverty and disease.

This is an Italy of curious young people with dreams that are, perhaps, difficult for their parents to understand. What these young people need desperately to understand is that the glitz and glamour of America come at an awful price of over complicated living. For people like Marie Vero, Joe De Simone, and even Domenico from La Campagnola, that price was too high. All of them returned to Italy.

As Grazia talked, with wide eyes, about her dream to learn English and come to America, I could not help but miss the slight look of disapproval in the eyes of her parents, Marie and Vito. It was the same look that we would have given our own children.

The conversation turned to books. When I mentioned something about the memoir[20] I had written and published, Vito lit up like a hundred watt light bulb. He has written a few books himself. He literally jumped from his seat to fetch a copy of both[21] his published books so that he could present copies to us. He signed the books and presented them to us without even thinking twice. This common bond of "authorship" had brought us a little closer together, irrespective of the language barrier. Vito was absolutely beaming when he handed the books over.

The time was now 3:00 PM. We began to discuss a plan for the rest of the day. To us, the "rest of the day" is not quite

---

20 27 Cottage Place, copyright 2013, Peter Barbella, LOC number 2013923280

21 "Erculea Proles" and "Cavalieri E Vergini Guerriere" by Vito Tricarico published by Cultura Fresca and Vitale Edizione respectively

as long as an Italian "rest of the day". We expressed our desire to fulfill our mass obligation that evening[22], so we developed the following plan.

Illustration 90: Cimetero di Palo del Colle

First, since we had expressed a wish to visit the local cemetery, Vito was going to take us for a visit to the Palo del Colle cemetery. There was a slim chance that it was open and we might find some interesting facts there. Next, he would take us on a walk to find specific streets that we wanted to see. These were streets that were recorded on Italian civil records of Gay's ancestors that we had studied. So we knew Gay's ancestors had lived in homes on these streets. Even if the houses were gone, we wanted to see the streets.

This was going to be a fairly quick tour. Afterwards, we

22 Despite the fact that we had already attended a service this day, it was prior to noon. As a consequence, our weekend mass obligation remained unfulfilled.

were going to drive to Bari to see the city and we would attend mass there in a grand cathedral. I wondered how it would be possible to fit all that into one evening. Bari had to be at least a forty minute drive. Would we be able to get to Bari for a 4:00 PM or 5:00 PM mass. It was already past 3:00 PM. In any event we nodded ascent with the plan and we began with a walk to the cemetery.

Illustration 91: A Tricarico crypt

The cemetery was not far from Vito's home. It was at the end of a broad and very clean boulevard lined with deciduous trees. You could almost visualize a parade of mourners approaching the entrance, following a horse drawn cart bearing a deceased love one. In the silence of this particular evening I could, in my imagination, hear the creaking of the cart wheels carrying the casket as well as the soft footsteps of the mourners. I could hear the wailing of a somber hymn of sorrow in Gregorian Chant style. I have to admit that the early evening shadows were aiding in the look of solemnity that lay before us.

Illustration 92: Great Great Grandma lived on this street in Palo

When we walked all the way down the entrance road, we found that the cemetery was closed. We would not be able to go inside. However, you could see much of it from the front gate. It looked not unlike the cemetery we had seen in Sperone. It was very well kept and very bright, even in the late afternoon Italian sun. The predominant color of the crypts was white, adding to the overall brightness.

From the front entrance we spotted a Tricarico crypt and a Mastrandrea crypt. We could, however, not get close enough to identify any potential relatives. We took a few pictures to record our visit and walked on.

Our next goal was to go "street hunting". Vito marched us back past his house and right back to the old piazza in the central part of the town.

We walked along, noting ancestral streets, here and there. Vito brought us to Via Trappeti, corso Terra dei Greci and other streets which we had requested and as we walked, Vito pointed out other sights of old Palo del Colle. Finally we came to the location of the jewelry store where Michele Lattanzi had plied his trade. Michele had been a goldsmith, just as had his father and his grandfather back in old Bari.

Illustration 93: Sight of the former Lattanzi Jewelry store

As we walked the streets, we were struck by how excited Vito was to be showing us his town. He clearly had a great knowledge of his home and was delighted to be showing it off. His exuberance was catching. He rarely failed to point out this antiquity or that. The streets were very old and there were ample opportunities for him to show us ancient things.

The hours were passing by and I was wondering if somehow we had missed our opportunity to travel to Bari for mass. I reckoned that we had taken too much time walking about the town. At the same time, I was

Illustration 94: Another Ancestral Street

Illustration 95: Communal fountain, 1888

beginning to wonder if Vito and Marie had fully
understood our desire to attend an evening service. So,

when we noticed the people congregating at Palo del Colle's mother church of Santa Maria La Porta right there, in the square, for their Saturday evening mass, we suggested, to Vito, that this might be the right service for us to attend. We were here now, at the right place and at the right time.

While it was not the original plan, Vito was willing to bend over backwards to accommodate us. He understood our desire and he left us at the church to go for his wife. He told us he would be back with her soon. We entered the church to attend the 5:00 PM mass.

We were startled when we found a service already in progress, at least fifteen minutes early. Because of the language barrier, it took a while for us to recognize that this was not the mass service, but rather a pre-mass prayer service.

Although we were early for the mass, it was good to sit down after all the sightseeing the tireless Vito had provided. My feet were singing the blues and a nice quiet mass is just what the doctor ordered.

The church was dark and cool and after the 15 minute prayer service, the priest retired to the sacristy to prepare himself for the actual mass.

As time passed, more and more people began coming into the church. By the time the mass began, the church was fairly full. Vito and Maria had not shown up yet. We enjoyed being there in the cool church with the people of

Palo. It gave us a strange sense of togetherness with a people that we did not really know, yet somehow felt connected to. We wanted to be off the beaten path, and that's where we were.

Illustration 96: Mass at Santa Maria La Porta in Palo del Colle

A few minutes after the mass began, Vito and Maria showed up and sat in the pew behind us. We worshiped in solidarity. It was clear that the Catholic mass was as important to Vito and Marie as it is to Gay and I. In all three places we have been so far, the church in Italy plays a far more significant role in society than it does in the states. Was this another of the many cultural differences we were observing? I wondered about that.

When the mass was completed, I asked Vito and Marie if they would like to join us at Masseria Vero for dinner. Despite the fact that this was not the original plan, after a brief consultation with his wife, Vito accepted. Bari would wait for another day.

We walked back to the Tricarico house and invited the rest of the family as well. Domenico accepted our invitation so we drove, in two cars out to Masseria Vero and Marie fed us a dinner in what seemed like a thousand courses.

We sat for a good long time at table, and with the help of Marie Vero and Domenico we managed to communicate fairly well. We talked about many things. I inquired how Vito had met Maria. He said they worked together in Northern Italy when he was young. Vito was a customs agent on the Italy/France border before he retired and came home to Palo del Colle. We talked about Domenico's teaching position in a nearby town. We talked about the the excitement being generated by the coming wedding of their daughter, Anna.

Illustration 97: Domenico, Gay, Maria, and Vito at Masseria Vero

It was quite late when we said our final farewell to Vito and his wife. Domenico had mentioned that he would like to show us some of the sights of Bari and Bitonto. He offered to give us a tour the next day, Sunday, but I wasn't sure he was committed to doing that for us. What young man would want to spend his entire Sunday guiding a couple of geriatrics through Italian cities. In any event, we said goodbye, and then, totally exhausted, Gay and I retired for the evening. Whatever Sunday's plan would be, it would be spontaneous and perhaps serendipitous but it was going to have to wait for a much deserved deep sleep.

Giovinazzo, Bari and a Real Cousin

Illustration 98: One of a variety of flowers on the farm

This time we were expecting it. That didn't make it easier to take, but when the donkey began his morning braying, we were kind of prepared. Once again, the donkey woke up the rooster and the geese. The animal symphony brought us to the realization that another day was dawning and we were about to continue our Italian adventure.

We pulled ourselves from our comfortable bed, tidied our room and got ready for whatever the new day would bring.

Illustration 99: Another morning brought to us by the animal symphony

Breakfast was another feast put on by Marie. She scrambled up more eggs for us and now, she knew how we liked our coffee, in a large cup with a lot of hot water. There was also biscotti, toast with jam and Nutella. We took our time at breakfast chatting with Marie. We talked about her time in the US when she was younger. She enjoyed her stay in the states, but she knew her place was here, at home, in Palo. Somehow, from our current vantage point, it was easy to see the wisdom in her decision to return home.

After breakfast, we took a little walk around the grounds.

Curious about the animals who were providing us the morning music, we strolled by the shed and looked in at them. To no one's surprise, the animals looked back at us, as if to say, "you guys are a long way from home, aren't you?".

We stopped at each place where we spotted a flower that looked different from the flowers we were accustomed to. There were many which we recognized, but quite a few extraordinary species that were foreign to us.

Illustration 100: The grazing herd

We could look out over the broad fields to see the sheep

and goats grazing in a pasture adjacent to the olive grove. Although I'm sure the animals were making some type of noise, in the distance, we could hear nothing but an eerie silence, lending to the quiet of the farm.   The olive trees themselves seemed to go on for miles and miles in neat little rows.

Illustration 101: Fig trees go on forever

Behind the farm we found what appeared to be fig trees with a unique protection system. Each tree had a dog tied up to it. While I'm sure these dogs would be fierce competitors against any fig tree predator (whatever that might be), they seemed quite docile with us. They were as curious about the "crazy Americani" roaming the grounds, as were the farm hands who were busily carrying out the daily chores of the farm.

Also, directly behind the farm was a recreation area which looked completely out of place here, lending a Never Never Land atmosphere to the farm.

Illustration 102: Main pool at the farm

Here, on this farm, out in the country, was an extensive water recreation area. Standing there, looking at it, we had to pinch ourselves to believe what we were seeing. This enormous tiled area featured three separate pools complete with waterfalls. The main pool was at least twenty five yards long and was shaped in a figure eight. The other pools were meant for younger people and were smaller.

Marie explained that she used the pool area in the summer for groups of disadvantaged youth. In any event, it was early enough in the season that the pools did not contain water yet. Otherwise, they looked so inviting, I would have been shopping for a bathing suit. This exotic water paradise couldn't have seemed stranger, flanking the fig and olive trees, but there it was.

We meandered back to the front of the farmhouse only to find a great surprise; visitors waiting for us in the lobby. Remember the friend we made in the old piazza in Palo, Giacomo Mittaritona? He was the man who said he would call a Lattanzio and let her know we were at the farm. Well, he did just that. And, to our amazement, Angela Lattanzio was so excited to hear the news that an American cousin was in town that she drove from the village to the farm with her husband, Domenico Amendolara just to see and meet the "strange Americani". Here they were, sitting in the lobby, waiting for us. How exciting is this?

Illustration 103: Gay with cousin Angela Lattanzio and her husband, Domenico Amendolara

We had a wonderful time simply introducing ourselves and discussing family. Angela had brought pictures of her Grandparents and Uncles and Aunts. We took notes and photos of all the pictures she had brought with her. We shared what we knew of our family histories[23]. Angela

23 At the time of Angela's visit, Gay and I were not 100% sure that

explained that her father was Vito and that she, herself, was named after her nonna.

Illustration 104: The Lattanzio family of Palo del Colle

So, after we exhausted our conversation with Angela and Domenico, we exchanged email addresses with promises of future correspondence. As we were doing this, in walks Domenico Tricarico, ready to give us a private tour of Giovinazzo and Bari. Domenico had a huge smile on his face. It was easy to see that he was excited about showing us his knowledge of the history of the area. We said arrivederci to the Lattanzios and were off on a private tour with Domenico. This new adventure was about to consume the remainder of the day.

Angela and Gay were bonafide cousins. However, since our return from Italy, we have confirmed that indeed they are. Both Angela and Gay share a great grandfather, Michele Lattanzio who was the family Goldsmith. Michele was born and raised in Bari, but moved to Palo del Colle after he was married.

Off to the Adriatic Sea

We climbed into Domenico's car, and left the farm to the farmers. Once again it was impossible to follow all the turns that were required to come out of the country and get on a paved highway. What would we do without the wonderful Tricarico family to take us in and out of this magical place.

While Domenico had originally told us that we were going to visit the town of Bitonto, we actually went a little further to the coastal town of Giovinazzo. Giovinazzo, originally

founded by the Romans, was an important trading partner with the city of Venice. Once there, we found ourselves in the presence of buildings and streets which were created as early as the 2nd century (AD).

Are you kidding? This is crazy. These buildings are six

Illustration 105: Ancient column from the 2nd Century (AD)

times older than George Washington would be today if he were still alive. Here we are standing next to them. "No big deal", you say? Try it. Stand in the presence of one or more of these antique structures, and see if you don't feel the sense of awe that we did.

Two of the oldest buildings in the town are its cathedral and its ducal palace. Domenico was sure to take us to both of them.

Illustration 106: Cathedral of Giovinazzo

Domenico told us that the Cathedrale of Giovinazzo[24] was endowed by a French princess in 1113 and completed in 1180, some 67 years later. One wonders if the princess lived to see the finished project. While parts of this church have been rebuilt, original sections remain and they are in remarkable condition considering their proximity to the

---

24 To read, verbatim, the plaque attached to the Cathedrale, see Appendix II.

sea, just a short distance behind it.

We also visited the Ducal Palace of Giovinazzo[25]. This
building was constructed to provide defense of the harbor
in the mid 17th century. The northern facade, shown in the
illustration was built on top of the ancient town walls. You
can see the line which separates the old and the new,
marked by the different types of blocks in illustration 107.

Illustration 107: Ducal Palace of Giovinazzo

We visited ancient site after site. Domenico showed us the
12th century Chiesa San Andrea, the 16th century Palazzo
Marziani and the 14th century Palazzo Siciliano. We were
overwhelmed with antiquity.

We walked and walked, and walked seeing many other
interesting sights. There were magnificent ocean views

25 To read, verbatim, the plaque attached to the Ducal Palace, see
   Appendix III.

featuring harbors of boats and expansive beaches. Finally we returned to the cathedral. Since it was lunch time and we were hungry, we found a nice bar to have a little lunch. It was early afternoon at this point.

We ordered three different menu items and shared them among ourselves. Each of the sandwiches we ordered were local favorites and each was better than the other, if that is possible. We topped the meal with an amazing chocolate gelato that made us forget just how tired our feet were. It was good to sit for a little while, for now we were back in the car and on our way to the city of Bari for another round of amazing history and sights.

Illustration 108: Ancient castle in the city of Bari

Our first stop in Bari was the ancient city palace. Here, within its protected walls lived the nobles and important craftsmen of the city. Among those was Gay's great great Grandfather, Sabino Lattanzio, the city goldsmith. He had learned his trade from his father, Natale, and had passed it on to his son, Michele. Anything in the city of Bari that involved gold passed through their hands.

We walked and walked as Domenico enthralled us with his knowledge of the area. He took us to a place where an old Roman road had been uncovered during a construction project. This was the Piazza del Ferrarese. The construction was stopped immediately and re-planned so that the road would be preserved for all to see. Imagine looking at a roadway that preceded the time of Christ.

Illustration 109: An original Roman road

We walked all around Bari seeing one sight after the other. There was an amazing contrast between the ancient city and the modern city. Here in the modern city we found a bust of Nicola Petrovic, the father-in-law of Vittorio Emmanuele.[26] Nicola was the prince of Montenegro across

---

26 In this era, daughters of royalty were often promised to royalty

the Adriatic from Bari. The bust was placed here to note the cordial relations between the two great kingdoms.

We went back into the old section and there we encountered a plaque, written in Latin, honoring Carolus Bourbonius, the Bourbon king who drove the Austrians from this area, leading to the Kingdom of the two Sicilies. It is so amazing to be surrounded by this history which we have been studying for so long. Words cannot express how wonderful it was to be taking all this history in first hand.

Illustration 110: Mother church - old Bari

We finally ended up in the mother church of the old city. At this point it was late afternoon. A mass was in progress, and I was exhausted from all the walking. My head was taking 911 calls from my feet. This was about as far as my walking parts were going to walk this day.

We looked about the church and then Domenico went to fetch the car. He drove it right into the church piazza to pick us up. It felt good to sit down and drive back to the farm.

---

from neighboring countries, as a method of keeping up good will and peace.

We persuaded Domenico to dine with us at the farm. We sat down and enjoyed another one of Marie's fabulous feasts. We talked about the day and all the fabulous historical sites we had taken in together. We couldn't get over this 35 year old young man taking his entire Sunday to show us around. Grazie mille was inadequate. We simply couldn't thank him enough.

At the end of the evening, the conversation switched to our next day's adventure. We were going to visit the village of Trani, up the coast from Bari, and then we were headed for Rocco San Giovanni, near Chieti. However, our first task was going to be finding our way out of the countryside to a known highway.

Illustration 111: Pete with Domenico

Domenico gave us specific instructions on how to do this. He explained how to get off the farm and how to find the best route to the village of Trani. He even drew a map to assist us. Domenico has to be one of the kindest and most patient people in Italy. We finally said farewell, and retired for our last evening on the farm. Dead tired, we collapsed in our bed and retained consciousness for less than one second.

On to Trani

Oh No! Hey guys, we're tired. Could you cut us a little slack this morning? No way! The animal symphony once again broke the silence at an ungodly hour. However, it was all for the best because we had a busy Monday planned.

Illustration 112: Animal Symphony - the altos

Today, our first stop is to the division of the Bari Archivio di Stato located in the coastal town of Trani. This is where the civil records of Palo del Colle are stored. This is where we hoped to explore Tricarico records which might not be available online. We hoped to spend a little time there before we pushed on to our next town. As a secondary objective, we wanted to connect with the Archive officials for potential future correspondence.

We got up, washed up and went down to one more breakfast feast. I think Marie saved the best for last. We made small talk with another couple that had arrived at the farm. They were from northern Italy, and here to visit relatives. The previous day they had witnessed our reunion with Angela Lattanzio and they were curious about our adventures. We told them our tale of adventure.

Then we went out to say good by to the animals, the farmhands, and Marie and Domenico.

Illustration 113: Following Domenico out to the highway

We were in the middle of our farewells with all the farm folk when who should walk into the farm house but Domenico Tricarico. Apparently he had been quite concerned as he gave us departure directions and drew maps last night. He recognized the glazed look in my eyes as he was explaining how we should proceed to Trani. He decided to spend his Monday morning leading us out of the wilderness and onto the correct highway just to make sure we got started off on the right foot. Without a doubt, this young man is a gem.

We, of course, accepted Domenico's kind offer and then settled our bill. We packed the FIAT and with one last arrivederci, we were ready to leave. We began the last phase of our adventure.

I was very glad to hear the FIAT diesel engine kick over, because this is the first time we had used it since we arrived at the farm. It had sat unused for almost three days collecting olive and fig pollen. Luckily, our FIAT was white so we could not detect any other things that may have been deposited there. We formed a two car caravan and began to find our way out of the farmlands.

Domenico got us out of the country and on to a main road where Sophia located some satellites. Now we were, once again, in her hands. With one more farewell and heartfelt thank you, we were on our way.

Our trip to Trani was uneventful, yet scenic. It took us a little less than an hour to drive north on the highway. We made the appropriate exit and drove directly to the

Illustration 114: Cloudless sky in Trani

coast. We were told that Trani was a pretty village. We, indeed, found a lovely coastal village whose buildings were radiant white.

The sun had finally made a full appearance. This was our first cloudless and rainless day. It was gorgeous. The sky was colored a brilliant blue that is hard to describe as we drove into Trani, and it gave the buildings a spotlessly clean look.

Illustration 115: Gay enters the Trani Archivio di Stato

We found a piazza near the Archivio di Stato. We were unsure about the status of the parking spaces; pay or free. We asked a passerby and with a little help from hand gestures we determined that we could purchase a parking permit in the local bar across the piazza or we could purchase the permit from any uniformed pollizioto. We found a man in a uniform selling the parking tags to place on the dashboard of our car. He seemed legitimate, so we purchased a card for four hours and went off to find the Archives.

We weren't sure what we were going to find here in the Archives. We knew that most of the civil records from Palo del Colle were already available on line. I suppose we wanted to see if there were some records which were not available elsewhere. In any event, we entered the archives, introduced ourselves, and once again, we were treated like royalty.

We met with the staff in the Archives and we discussed our goal of finding a few records of Tricaricos and Lattanzios. The head genealogist there, signor Mauro Elia Di Pinto looked over the dates we were interested in and dispatched a clerk to fetch records. We did find a few interesting records, but more importantly, we made contact with staff who could prove to be valuable partners in the

Illustration 116: Staff at Trani Archives

future.

After several hours of research it was time to move on to

our next stop. We had not exhausted all the records we
might have researched, but we wanted to move on to our
next B&B in the village of San Rocca Giovanni before it got
too dark. We thanked the staff and made our way back to
the car.

On the way, we stopped for a moment or two to simply
take in the breathtaking view of the sea and the beautiful
blue sky. (azzuro, azzuro) It was not easy leaving this
place.

Illustration 117: Church in Trani - just beyond is the Adriatic Sea

We got into the FIAT and asked Sophia to take us to our
next stop, another agriturismo called Rifugiomare. This
"refuge on the sea" was located in the small coastal village
of Rocca San Giovanni in the Chieti province. We selected
this B&B based on the recommendation of "computer
cousin" Antonella Barbella who was born and raised in

this area. It was ideally located halfway between the village of Vasto where my paternal Grandmother was born, and the city of Chieti. The Archivio di Stato which holds the records of Vasto is located in Chieti. Antonella is an internationally known chef and through social media, we have become friends. She gave glowing recommendations for the owners of Rifugiomare, Bepe and Brunetta, who we were about to meet.

The trip up the coast was a little more than 200 miles. It was a picture perfect day. We stopped for some lunch at an Auto-Grill and we ate our food under the crystal clear blue sky. We sat at a picnic table and munched on more interesting local pizza and a little water. It was pleasant there in the shade, watching the people come and go.

Illustration 118: Small Commune along the way

Getting back into the FIAT, we continued our trip. We drove by one small town after another along the way on the AutoStrada, and like our trip across the country from

Sassano to Bari, the landscape was speckled with numerous hills and wind turbines.

When Sophia directed us to leave the AutoStrada, we found ourselves on a smaller coastal road, heading north to Rocco San Giovanni. There was some road construction to contend with which made us feel like we were back in the states, but we were doing alright. Remarkably, we were drawing a significantly reduced amount of horns from irate native drivers. The road along the Adriatic Sea was simply wonderful; not unlike California's Pacific Coast Highway. To our left the land sloped up. To our right, the Adriatic Sea, whose crystal clarity nearly matched the blue sky, went on to the horizon. We were driving along famously, that is, until Sophia asked us to make a left turn off this magical coast road.

Gay and I looked at each other in disbelief at the path Sophia wanted us to follow. It's not that the road was unusually constrictive, although to be sure, the road was indeed narrow. The problem was that this road seemed to be going up about an eighty degree incline. I wasn't at all sure that the FIAT engine was powerful enough to get us up this hill.

There wasn't much we could do. Sophia was in command at this point and there seemed no reasonable alternative. I put the FIAT in first gear and began the hair raising ascent.

Up we went, almost feeling more like we were in a roller coaster car than in a FIAT. While driving at this frightening angle we encountered several hairpin turns,

placed there presumably to make for a reduced incline.
Without the hairpins, would this have been a vertical
incline? Thank God there were no cars coming down the
hill.

Eventually, the trusty FIAT got us to the top of the
mountain, but now, Sophia said (more or less) "this is as
far as I can take you". You see, Sophia accepted the street
we had programmed her with, but she did not recognize
the house number[27]. We still didn't see Rifugiomare.

Illustration 119: Patio of Rifugiomare

We were on the correct street, but we were at a T in the
road with just a 50% chance of guessing correctly which
way to turn. We turned right, and fortunately, that was the
proper direction, but soon the road turned to dirt and
stones and began a steep descent. What goes up must

---

27 Note to self: Get Sophia a new "wardrobe" when we return to
   America.

come down.

After about a quarter kilometer, we spotted a man, standing there in his yard. We asked if he knew where Rifugiomare was. He looked at me quizzically and obliviously wasn't sure, but he knew there was a fancy place further down the road. He thought it might be the place we were looking for.

Illustration 120: The rooms of this B&B are directly beneath the grass you see in this picture. We told all our friends that we slept "under the grass"

So down we went, continuing our descent, perhaps halfway back down the hill we had just climbed. As the slope of the descent increased, I was beginning to think dark thoughts about cousin Antonella, wondering if we were going to need to rent a donkey to take us the rest of the way. Finally, we arrived at the backside of an elongated building along the side of the hill. There we spotted a "Rifugiomare" sign. We pulled into the parking area and we couldn't believe our eyes.

Here was a paradise that we knew we were not going to want to leave. Here, instead of thinking about pins and voodoo dolls of Antonella, we turned around 180 degrees and began singing her praises. We sat there with our mouths agape, just staring at the beauty before us. Between the sky and the sea, there was more concentrated blue than we could cope with. The land below ran down to the Adriatic Sea and the visible hillside was peppered with olive trees.

We got out of the car and breathed what seemed like the cleanest air we had ever breathed. The bright blue sky did nothing to take away from the staggering magnificence before us.

The building was equally remarkable. We were standing in the parking area of a two storied structure. We were on the lower level which appeared to be reserved for guest rooms. The main house was on the upper level.

When we finished gaping at the sea, we took a deep breath and climbed the stairs to the main level to see about checking in. To our surprise, there was no one there ("Deja Vous all over again"[28]). That allowed us the opportunity to continue gaping at the beautiful scene from the upper level.

We walked about the upper patio for a short time,

---

28 Yogi Berra

alternating our glances between the landscape, the main building and the view. Rifugiomare is the home of Brunetta and Bepe. Brunetta is a very imaginative architect, and her creativity was evident as we looked over her home. The entire east side of her home was a beautifully appointed sun room. Her patio was creatively adorned and neatly landscaped.

We went back down the stairs to the car and took a look at the rooms on the lower level. They seemed very modern and very well appointed. However, they all seemed empty. Once again, we were to be the only occupants.

Illustration 121: Sun Room, overlooking the Adriatic

After a while we heard a car pull into the lot and we went back up the stairs to investigate. Here, we first met Brunetta, who had been out shopping. We introduced ourselves, and, indeed, Brunetta had been expecting us. She apologized for not being there when we arrived. We made fast work of checking in, and Brunetta showed us to our room below.

She unlocked the large wooden sliding door at the entrance to our room. It revealed a secondary glass door which afforded a beautiful view of the olive grove below the courtyard leading down to the ocean. The room was, as we had thought, very modern, very well appointed, and very clean. The walk in shower was the roomiest shower we had ever seen in Italy. We brought our bags in and set up house. I was annoyed with myself for only booking two days here.

Brunetta then invited us up to the main house for some coffee and cookies. She ushered us through her sun room into the main dining area. To make matters even better, Brunetta had an American coffee maker. Now we knew we were in heaven.

Brunetta served up some coffee with a large bowl of delicious cookies. She told us they were wine cookies[29]. Now this was something new and for us, who are weight challenged, potentially dangerous. Now we can get our alcohol and our desserts in one fell swoop. Could this be legal? I sat and ate the cookies like they were peanuts, mortifying Gay. And the coffee was wonderful as well.

We chatted for a while with Brunetta who knew a few words of English. It was early evening and we had no place special to go to, so we spent some time in this glorious sun room. We took stock of our last few days,

---

29 See Appendix VII for the recipe

caught up on some notes and duly recorded things in our computer.

As supper time was approaching, we asked Brunetta about a good local restaurant for dinner. It was almost 6:00 PM now. We were thinking about sampling some fresh fish from the Adriatic. Brunetta recommended Il Cavalluccio, a small restaurant near the bottom of the mountain. She called them for us to be sure that they were open and she told them we would be there shortly.

Illustration 122: Entrance to Il Cavallauccio

So we got in the FIAT and fearlessly began the trek down the mountain. If you can believe it, after we descended the steep hill safely, the driveway to Il Cavalluccio was a little steeper than the mountain road. We found ourselves, now, right on the beach. A tsunami would level this restaurant. We had to walk through some sand to reach the entrance.

We walked into the restaurant and it was apparently a little earlier than they were accustomed to having patrons. It was near 7:00 PM at this point, but the restaurant was empty. We seated ourselves next to a window and looked out at the sea. Somehow the vastness of the sea and the silence of the room complimented each other in a way that made the atmosphere special. We began to feel the pangs which accompany the end of a great experience. We were nearly finished with our Italian odyssey and we wanted to make the most of the remaining few days.

Eventually the waiter came along and left us a menu. After a brief discussion, we settled on a pasta seafood dish for two. We ordered a little wine and we had some bread to nibble on while we waited for the main course.

Illustration 123: Are we supposed to eat that thing?

The main course came and the pasta and the seafood were great, however, the seafood was not easy to get. It fought us every inch of the way. Virtually everything on the plate, excepting the pasta, had a shell of some sort. We had to work doubly hard to extract even small edible bits of the sea food. The food was good, but we were exhausted by the time we had finished. While we were eating, a group of men had come in, added some background noise and a little atmosphere to the restaurant. Prior to this, it had been easy to imagine that we were the only two people in Italy. The crowd noise seemed to take us out of that reverie.

We sat in the restaurant until the shadows began deepening and nightfall was imminent. We could see the lights of the boats out on the sea. We started thinking about our plans for the next day. We were going first, to the small village of Vasto, home of the DeCristofaros.[30] We were going to search for specific churches that we had discovered in various civil records. Tomorrow was Tuesday and the town offices should be open, so we were also going to try to see if there was any useful information in the Anagrafe Office. Vasto was located on the sea, about 20 miles south of Rifugiomare.

Then, if time permitted, we were going to get back in the car and head in the opposite direction, North to the City of Chieti. There we were going to spend some time in the Chieti Archivio di Stato which houses the civil records of Vasto. We also wanted to meet and personally thank Dr. Miriam Ciarmi. She had previously been very responsive to our requests and had already sent us a good deal of data via email.

---

30 Consiglia DeCristofaro was the husband of Francesco Barbella. They were my nonna and nonno.

We finalized our plans and then we settled our bill for the food and wine. We got into the FIAT and began the ascent back up the mountain. By the time we got back to Rifugiomare, Brunetta's partner had returned home and we joined the two of them in some polite conversation.

Both Brunetta and Bepe had some ability with English words. We discovered that Bepe was a furniture maker and he had done all of the doors, windows, and wooden furniture that we could see in his home. They were quite impressive. We found out that Brunetta and Bepe had met in this small coastal village.

We shared a little evening snack of cookies. Then, with a small glass of limoncello, we retired for the night. This had been a long and fruitful day. Even though the end of this adventure was in sight, we still had a lot to accomplish. This time, we were looking forward to a night of sleep without an early wake up symphony.

Vasto

This morning we woke up on our own account, without the assistance of an animal symphony. Just to make up for the last three days, we stayed in bed a little longer. After washing and dressing, we went upstairs to enjoy a wonderful breakfast spread put out by Brunetta and Bepe. There, under another brilliant blue Italian sky, we had eggs, blood orange juice, coffee, cake, cookies and bread. We did not leave the sun room/breakfast area hungry.

Illustration 124: Abruzzo, countryside

We collected our notes and necessary tools. Our plan for this day was to visit the Vasto Ufficio di Anagrafe and the Chieti Archivio di Stato.

The ride to Vasto was simply gorgeous, south, along the coastal highway. We got alternate glimpses of the ocean on our left and the inland farmlands and countryside on our right. Just north of the village, the scene began to turn more urban.

When we arrived in Vasto, we were surprised to find that it was far more than a small southern Italian commune. This was a modern city, not unlike many American towns. Although Vasto is considered to be a part of southern Italy, it seemed far more like a northern Italian community.

On our way to the Ufficio di Anagrafe, Sophia led us up a busy "main" type street peppered with businesses, shops, and some apartment style homes. It wasn't until we came near a very modern Vasto city hall that we encountered the intact old section of the town. Here, there was an amazing contrast of the old and the new. The divide between the two was sharp and distinct, as if city planners had drawn a line (which they probably did).

Illustration 125: Off to Vasto City Hall

Unlike other congested towns where parking was impossible, we easily found a place to park. There, right across the street from the city hall was a large, modern parking garage. We pulled in, took a ticket, parked the car in one of the many available spots, and headed over to the town hall.

We entered the city hall and spent just a few moments looking for the Anagrafe office. It was conveniently located. Highly visible signs led us right to the door. However, before we could reach that door we needed to get into one of the two very long lines snaking out from the office windows. It was not obvious if the two lines were there for two different purposes. We didn't want to get stuck on an automobile license line to ask a genealogy question.

Illustration 126: Old Vasto, across the street from a very modern city hall

Gay and I strategized and we resolved the problem easily.
We each got into one of the lines. No matter what
happened, one of us would be on the right line, hopefully.
My line went a little faster so I stepped up to the window
first.

I introduced myself to the official. I explained that we had
come from America to search for information about my
bisnonno, Rafaelle DeCristofaro, from Vasto. I then
showed him a pictorial representation of the DeCristofaro
family that I had with me. He gave me a rather pained
look. I could hear him thinking. You could imagine he
was muttering under his breath, "you've got to be kidding
me!! All I need on this busy day is some stupid Americano
asking me to help him look up dead people in our old
records. Heaven help me!" He looked at my family chart
for a second, then he thought for a moment, and explained,
politely, that I would be better off in the other line. He
simply wanted me to go bother the other, equally busy,
official.

No problem; Gay had held position in her line, and in a
few minutes, we were up to the window of the second
official. We introduced ourselves to the second official,
and gave him the same speech and request. I showed him
the family chart. This official gave me another pained
look. He rolled his eyes a little and looked at all the people
behind me. But this time, we got a slightly different
response.

The official looked down at the family chart for some time.
He looked up at us for some time. Then he said, yes, I will

help you, but look, we are very busy right now. If you come back around 12:30, I will help you.

We left the office. I was a little disappointed. I was skeptical that this official would even be there at 12:30, let alone help us. I had read accounts of people being brushed off by Anagrafe officials, and I thought this was going to be another example.

Illustration 127: Chiesa di San Giuseppe, Vasto

Never mind. We still wanted to look around the old town to see if we could find the Chiesa di San Giuseppe where some of my relatives had been baptized and married. Also, we wanted to see some more of the old town.

I made a plan adjustment. Now, we would look around the old town for a short time and then return to the car and move on to the Archivio di Stato in Chieti. Forget coming back to these two bureaucrats who just gave us the brush off. Gay would have none of my new plan. We came here to get help at the Anagrafe office and, by golly, we were going to get that help. She insisted that we come back to the Anagrafe office. Knowing her resolve, I made a wise choice in letting her have her way. It was around 10:30 AM. So we set off for a two hour tour of old Vasto.

Illustration 128: Cathedral di San Giuseppe

Outside the town hall I stopped a woman walking by and asked her if she knew where the chiesa di San Giuseppe was. To my surprise, she pointed to a church about 200 meters down the street from where we were standing.

We walked down the street to the church and there we had another surprise. The church was open. It was being cleaned by a cleaning crew. They did not stop us from entering. The Church was small, and quite plain, as Italian churches go. Given the warmth of the late morning sun, the church was astonishingly cool. The cleaning ladies went about their business as we took in the sights of the walls, the arches, the paintings, and the beautiful altar. The sunlight streaming through the large high windows bounced off the walls giving the church a bluish hue.

We spent a few moments in the coolness of the church. It was peaceful there. We dedicated a few prayers to the DeCristofaros and then we continued our exploration.

Our next goal was to find Via Francesco Assisi. We had identified this as the street that some of my relatives lived on. I remembered some advice from a fellow traveler

Illustration 129: Scusami, conosci via San Francesco di Assisi?

about not missing an opportunity to sit down with some of the local retired men spending their afternoon on a bench in the city square. So I did just that. I sat down with some fine looking gentlemen and I joined the conversation, as best I could. I then inquired about the location of Via Francesco Assisi. They directed me to the other side of the buildings in the piazza, not far away.

Illustration 130: Walking the streets of my genitori

We set out to look. We walked around the buildings lining the square and although we did not find it at first, with the help of another passer-by we were able to find the street.

Long and narrow, Via Francesco Assisi ran from the old part of the town down to the sea. It was marked, at its end with the Chiesa di San Francesco di Assisi. This church had the look of an abandoned building, but looked very different when we surprisingly found it open and went inside. This may have been the most ornate church we had seen on our adventure.

Upon entering, we were astonished at the paintings and carvings within. We were the only ones in the church. It was an honor to sit there where we knew so many had come before us.

Illustration 131: The ornate Chiesa di San Francesco di Assisi -
Vasto

I found a nameplate on one of the pews with the name
Trivelli, inscribed. That was the name of my father's
maternal grandmother. I wondered if there were family
still here in town There must be. That will have to be the
object of another visit, for now , it was almost 12:30, and
time for us to find our way back to the town hall to find
out how sincere that Anagrafe official really was.

The Foglio di Famiglia

We made our way through the streets of the old village
back to the Anagrafe office. Once again there was a line of
customers, but, this time the line was much smaller. We
got into the line that was being administered by the
official who promised to help. When we reached the
official and it was our turn, I fully expected him to tell us

that he could not find anything.

Instead, he rose from his seat and called on one of his coworkers to take charge of the line. He asked us to come with him. He ushered us into a back room.

There, he produced a Foglio di Famiglia for, not only my grandfather, Rafaelle DeCristofaro, but also for my great grandfather, Nicola DeCristofaro. I almost fell over in disbelief. The Foglio di Famiglia is a very special genealogical document.

Illustration 132: Nicola's foglio di famiglia

The Foglio di Famiglia is like a US census. It lists the names of everyone living in the family. It lists the names of their mothers and fathers. It lists the relationship of everyone to the head of the house. It lists the dates of their births (and deaths if appropriate) as well as their occupations. What an amazing find!

To get a sense of just how spectacular this find was, you have to understand that in Vasto, the name DeCristofaro is a little like the name Smith in the US. This official only looked at my family chart for a few moments. In that short time he was able to pinpoint my family out of all the other DeCristofaros in his records. How did he do this?

Clearly, this man knew more things about my family than I was able to extract from him with the time I had. We spent that time taking photos of the records he had found. He asked for no payment. To my regret, I never found out this man's name, but I wouldn't at all be surprised if it was DeCristofaro.

I thanked the man as much as I could. He was clearly a very busy official or else I would have stayed and tried to find out what else he knew. Again, this must be the object of another trip.

We left the town hall with a new appreciation of the treasures in local Anagrafe offices. We found our car in the parking garage, and it was time to head to Chieti. We had a little trouble getting out of the parking garage. We failed to notice[31] a sign which directed motorists to pay for their parking at a machine before proceeding to the gate (how American is that?). As a result, we found ourselves next to a card reader by the exit gate. The reader had no slot for a ticket and gate would not open for us. After we drew the ire of several motorists behind us, we were rescued by the attendant who explained how we were supposed to pay for our parking.

Finally we got out of the garage and we were on our way. But first, Gay had spotted a sign which read McDonald's further back on the road. This was an opportunity we were not going to miss.

---

31 Truthfully, if I had seen the sign, I probably would not have known what it was saying.

Illustration 133: A touch of America in Vasto

Where there's a McDonald's, there must be a real American cup of coffee. So off we went to find the Vasto McDonald's restaurant. It wasn't easy, but we found the prize. Parking was nonexistent so I more or less kept the car running as I double parked while Gay ran in to buy a few coffees. She came out with a large (small by any American standard) cup of coffee for me and a cappuccino for herself. We were in heaven for a little bit. We found a place to pull over and enjoyed this special treat. Then it was on to our next adventure.

On to Chieti

Illustration 134: Mount Maiella

The city of Chieti lies about 65 km north of Vasto. This ride was going to take us a little more than an hour, so we got on the AutoStrada. We drove for a while, and then, because it was near noon, we stopped at a convenient Auto-Grill for lunch. We had (what else) a couple of slices of the local variety of pizza and a drink, and then we put ourselves in the hands of Sophia.

The highway was picturesque and the countryside was beautiful. To our left loomed a massive mountain which I later learned was Mount Maiella. Although it looked as though it were near enough for us to reach out and touch, it was obviously very far away. Its position in my field of view remained constant almost all the way to Chieti.

When we reached the city, we encountered some bothersome Salerno style traffic and more narrow roads. Sophia had us zigging and zagging through the streets. When she finally announced that we had arrived, we could see no building which had the look of an official government office. There was no state archive in sight. What we saw appeared to be a row of apartment houses built along a hillside.

We asked a young man who fortuitously spoke excellent English, if he knew where the Archivio di Stato was. He listened to our question, delivered in Rosetta Stone Italian, and without asking where we were from, he replied, in perfect English[32], "yes, it is right over there." He pointed us at a stairway to a rather large nearby building.

We thanked him and climbed the stairs. There was a small sign on our right which clearly marked the entrance to the Archivio di Stato. We missed this sign completely. There was a series of pathways to different buildings. We walked on the pathway to the left, oblivious to the sign, and as a result, we found ourselves inside a private apartment house, looking for a door with an Archivio sign on it.

We climbed a few sets of stairs looking for any sign of the Archivio, and found none. After more fruitless searching Gay headed up another floor and I knocked on a nearby door. A young woman came to open it and gave me a suspicious look. I asked her if this was the Archivio di

32 It was exasperating to be spotted as an American so easily. I have made one of my personal goals to be mistaken as a real Italian some day, somewhere.

Stato. She looked at me like I had two heads. She let us know that this was a private residence hall. I gathered Gay from a few floors above and sheepishly we walked out of this building. Just as sheepishly we noticed the Archivio sign directing us to the correct door.

We then entered the Archivio and checked in at the front desk. Once more, we were greeted like royalty. There were three people working there. Each was more anxious than the other to help us find records of the DeCristofaro family.

There were two women and one man. We introduced ourselves and explained what we were looking for. We also asked if Miriam Ciarmi was working this day. Miriam is a young woman who had graciously sent me several records of my family, earlier, using email. I was hoping to thank her personally.

We talked with the staff about their holdings. From their listing of records it was easy to identify several books of data that we would like to see. The ladies took our request. The man went to fetch the appropriate records.

While he was retrieving the data, the women gave us a tour of their very modern facility. They were anxious to show it off to us. Here all the records are stored in controlled temperature and humidity. We got to see several floors of shelves stacked with some extremely old volumes.

The ladies, upon noticing my cognome, Barbella, also

suggested that we visit the Constantino Barbella museum of art which was only a kilometer away in the heart of the city. They showed us a book which described the museum

Illustration 135: With the staff at the Chieti Archivio di Stato

and they gave us directions.

When the man returned with several books of civil records, we poured over the data. We managed to successfully find a few items, including the original birth record of my great grandfather. That was satisfying.

Then, knowing that we wanted to thank Dr. Ciarmi, the women led us to a private office where they made a phone call to her. They allowed me to thank her over the phone. I was grateful for that opportunity. Dr. Ciarmi was very gracious and apologized for not being there that day to meet us.

As we left the Archivio, we decided that there was a little extra time to visit the art museum. We took the challenge to find it using the instructions we had received, but, alas, although we got within walking distance, we could not find a place to park the car. Literally, the streets were packed with small cars and scooters. Reluctantly, we gave up and asked Sophia to bring us back to Rifugiomare.

We drove back on the AutoStrada and then onto the now familiar coastal road to Rocca San Giovanni. If you can believe it, we were beginning to get used to the steep and narrow roadways.

Back in our room, we freshened up and then went upstairs to dinner. Bruna cooked us some fresh fish and Bepe made an elegant waiter. Between the

Illustration 136: Host Brunetta Bucciarelli in the kitchen

food and the wonderful homemade wine, we felt like royalty. We sat there eating our fish dinner and looking out over the sea. I'm sure heaven is a really nice place, but this was kind of nice also.

Illustration 137: Fresh (Adriatic Sea) fish for dinner

After dinner, Bepe and Bruna sat down and chatted with us. We enjoyed this more than the dinner. It is so nice to be with people who are so wonderful. We talked about everything, from childhood to politics. The language barrier was minimal because both Bepe and Bruna knew more English than we knew Italian.

After a while, nightfall fell and Bepe asked us to follow him outside. He wanted to show us something special. We went out the side door, and there in the dark was a stunning display of fireflies. I do not have the the ability to adequately describe this spectacle with pen alone. The fireflies were a little different than the ones we were used to. They were a little larger. But the striking thing was the sheer number of them. There in front of us were literally thousands of fireflies putting on a light show, the likes of which we had never seen. This was the perfect way to end our stay on Italy's east coast.

Illustration 138: Brunetta and Bepe

Sulmona

Today we woke up with mixed feelings of sadness and anticipation. We have been here, in Italy, for almost two weeks now and it is going to feel really good to return home. Yet, we have been on an incredible adventure. It will be bittersweet to see our odyssey end. We have seen wonderful places, made exciting discoveries and found new friends everywhere we have been. We know we must return, but some small part of us wishes that this dream could go on and on.

Brunetta and Bepe prepared another wonderful breakfast for us, and we sat for a while enjoying the beautiful view of the Adriatic. As we were settling our bill, Bepe excused himself to go off to his job. We said our goodbyes and went down to pack the FIAT to prepare it for the ride back toward Rome. While it is time to go, we have one more important stop to make. Our next stop will be in a small village, half way to Rome, to meet with some old friends.

We first met Peter and Anna Ventresca in our small hometown of Littleton, Ma. Peter and I were colleagues in the same company. Peter, a native Italian obtained dual citizenship when he retired. He then proceeded to build a home in his hometown. We were delighted to have the opportunity to see him and Anna again. We had previously made arrangements, by email, to visit them in their new home close to the village of Sulmona. Sulmona is about half way between Chieti and Rome so this was a convenient stop for us.

Peter had given us instructions to set our GPS to the small commune of Vallelarga which was near his home. So with a little effort, Sophia accepted our commands and we were off.

Illustration 139: Gay with Peter and Anna Ventresca

The ride across Italy to Sulmona was wonderful. Unlike our cross country trip further south, there were many snow capped mountains in view. Once we left the AutoStrada, the road seemed to blend seamlessly into the countryside. Traffic was light and the road was wide. We were enjoying the ride secure in the knowledge that we were not being tailgated by angry drivers.

We were approaching our way point, Vallelarga. I began to wonder how I would find Peter's home from wherever the GPS landed us. When the GPS said, "arriving at destination", I stopped the car. I assumed that in the absence of a street address Sophia had landed us somewhere in the middle of Vallelarga.

I needed to find someone to ask for help. I looked around at all the old homes searching for someone. The only person in sight was standing on a corner about 300 meters away. At first, I did not recognize him. Then, I blinked in amazement. The person standing on the corner was none other than Peter Ventresca, standing in the sunshine waiting for us to arrive. After the requisite greeting I just had to ask, "Peter, how long have you been standing here?" Peter answered, "Oh, about 10 minutes." Somehow, Peter knew exactly where the GPS was going to take me. I just love it when a plan comes together.

Illustration 140: Roman aqueduct in Sulmona

Peter led us to his home which is, to say the least, quite a magnificent palace. There we were greeted by his wife, Anna. Peter showed us the grounds, including his handmade rock maps of Italy and Massachusetts. He showed us all the rooms inside. He showed us the outdoor kitchen that was being finished by several workers.

We sat and caught up on old times. After we talked ourselves up to the present, Peter and Anna took us on a tour of the village of Sulmona. There we came to a very extensive and bustling open market. We saw an old town brimming with shops and markets of all types. There was an ancient Roman aqueduct running through the the center of the town. There were many other very old structures. It was late afternoon so Peter and Anna treated us to lunch at a very nice downtown Sulmona restaurant.

Illustration 141: Gay and Anna in Sulmona

We returned to their home and had a wonderful time chatting about family and common friends. Finally, we decided it was time to continue our trip towards Rome. Peter and Anna wanted to make sure we would not get lost, so they got in their car to lead us to the correct highway.

The Last Stop

Peter and Anna drove us all the way to the AutoStrada and we said our farewells. We made a promise to get together when they next came to the US. Their next trip was only a month away. Then we were on our way towards Rome, zipping along the AutoStrada.

Our last stop was in the small commune of Frascati on the outskirts of Rome. The logic which led me to this location seemed good when I made the reservation, but turned out to be not the best choice.

I wanted to avoid driving directly to the airport in Rome, ditching the rental car there, and then, taking a cab or train or bus to some hotel within the city limits near the airport. Such a plan would have incurred transportation charges to and from a hotel.

That extra charge led me to believe that it would be better to stay at a less expensive hotel on the outskirts of Rome. This plan B would have us driving to the outskirts, staying overnight, and taking the car to the airport the next morning to catch our flight.   Little did I know that there are several hotels right next to the airport where I could have ditched my Fiat. We could have taken advantage of free shuttles to the gates. Oh well; full speed ahead to Frascati.

So it is that we found ourselves on the AutoStrada, getting closer and closer to Rome, looking for Frascati. The traffic density was increasing by the second. Things were getting more and more hectic. Suddenly, Sophia was shouting out, "Uscita, Uscita," when clearly, there was no exit to be found (thanks to some ongoing road work). Now, having passed my exit, what do I do?

I got off the very next exit and Sophia told me, "Recalculating," then she barked "Fatto unooooo." What? It took me a while to understand that she wanted me to make a U turn.

Illustration 142: Il Paridiso - Bed and Breakfast (and other)

We made a successful U turn, got back on the AutoStrada, and headed in the other direction. After getting off the next exit we executed a number of confusing turns on very busy streets. After, what seemed like an eternity, we found ourselves on a narrow back alley. Sophia was saying, "arriva." But we did not see a sign for our B&B, Il Paridiso.

I did, however, spot a storefront which I seemed to recall from some of our early trip research with Google pictures. I didn't know what this store was, but I found a place to get the FIAT out of the way of traffic in the alley. I got out of the car, and went inside to see if they could help me find "Il Paridiso".

Illustration 143: Spacious driveway at Il Paridiso

The store was a pool hall and bar combination. It was rather shabby and somehow it advertised Soccer[33]. To my surprise, this "store" was also a Bed and Breakfast. This WAS Il Paridiso. That was only astonishing because I could not imagine where rooms might be.

---

33 It turned out that there was a small soccer field behind the store.

After confirming our reservation, I asked where are the rooms. A young man told me to drive up a narrow alleyway to the rooms behind (and above) the storefront. When I complained how narrow the driveway was, the young man gave me a quizzical look. With that one look, he was questioning my driving capabilities. He was also letting me know that there was plenty of room for the car to pass.

I got into the Fiat and cautiously made my way up the narrow driveway to a narrower parking spot which I had to share with a large motor scooter. We got out of the car and wondered if it would still be there in the morning. Such was the feel of the area we were in. I don't know why, but this seemed to be the scariest part of Italy we had ever been to.

Back in the store, (or restaurant, or pizzeria, or billiard hall; we weren't sure which) we registered. For the first time on our trip, it was suggested that we pay, up front. Hmmm! What type of B&B wants you to pay up front; oh never mind.

Well, I'm an optimistic sort, but still, I was getting a little nervous. In contrast to my minimal nervousness, my wife was in a full bout of apoplexy.

I paid the necessary 55 Euros, and a wiry little man, who looked more Arabic than Italian hoisted a huge ring of keys He led the way, up behind the store, behind a party room and down a narrow sidewalk to an upper section of the building which had a very heavy door. The door opened into a dimly lit hallway. Then he opened another heavy door to our room which was more dimly lit than the hallway.

Gay didn't say a word. She didn't have to. Her thoughts were coming through loud and clear. This was not like the bright, clean rooms that we had become accustomed to for the last two weeks. Still, we were very tired from our long drive and we were only a few short hours away from our trip to Rome's airport, Fiumicino, our last leg. So we shrugged our shoulders and decided to stay with the plan.

Neither of us was really hungry. We had, just a few hours ago, had a really nice meal with Peter and Anna. So we walked into the store and ordered two gelatos to try to settle our stomachs. A large man with a food stained apron took our order. He scooped a few small cups of gelato and took our money. We sat there for a while, watching the pool players. We felt Italian eyes staring at us, the two crazy Americani.

We finished our gelatos and retired for the night. As ridiculous as this sounds, I placed my heavy bag firmly against the door to slow down any possible forced entries. We washed up in the clean, but dinghy, bathroom. Gay took out her rosary beads to begin an all night novena. I actually don't know if she ever closed her eyes. With my wife on guard duty, I began fretting about the hectic ride into Rome, the next morning. After a few moments, I finally drifted off to sleep.

Sleep that night was fitful, but eventually the morning

came. We rose and dressed. We were delighted to see that our Fiat was still there. The red Honda was gone, but our car remained. We packed our bags for one final time and wheeled them out to the car. Then we walked down to the "dining room" to have our continental breakfast.

Illustration 144: The red motorbike is gone, but the FIAT is still here.

We made a new friend and some small talk with Marie, the pleasant woman who served our breakfast. The breakfast consisted of a tasty pastry and a cup of Italian coffee. I coerced Marie into pouring some hot water in the cup. She did not seem to understand why that was necessary.

Marie was quite interested in our adventure. We talked with her at length. It was obvious that Marie did not get to relate with a lot of Americans in her everyday life. Our visit was kind of special for her.

Illustration 145: Marie, head cook at Il Paridiso

We finished our breakfast, bid our adieus, and began our voyage into Rome. This wasn't the nicest place we stayed, but we survived to laugh about it.

But now; airport, here we come.

Home Sweet Home

Get Me To The Airport

OK! Here we go! This is our last drive in the FIAT. We are
so relieved that it is still in one piece. As long as I get to
the Hertz lot at the airport, without incident, there should
be no charges for unusual vehicle damage.

We got on the highway and started following Sophia's
instructions to Fiumicino. Sophia was clearly "on" this
morning. Her directions were impeccable despite the fact
that traffic was relentlessly heavy and fast. Sophia made
quick work of getting us on the main road to the airport.

Our stomachs settled a little when we began to see signs to
Fiumicino. We are almost there. This is our swan song in
the FIAT. Nevertheless we longed to see a sign directing
us to the Hertz return garage. Recall how underwhelmed
we were with the signs directing us to any auto rental
counter in the airport when we arrived. We were a little
nervous that we would encounter a similar lack of signs.
Thankfully, we were wrong. Gay spotted the first sign to
the Hertz car returns. From there, it was a piece of cake to
get the FIAT into the garage and parked.

When the attendant came over to us, I had him check the
car thoroughly. I wanted to be sure that Hertz agreed that
the car was returned in good condition[34]. I also showed

---

34 This insistence to be released from any auto damage obligations to
   Hertz arises from a long ago ugly incident in Hawaii which cost me
   $900.

him the defunct internet device. I told him it only worked for about twenty minutes. I requested and received a refund.

I have to admit to a considerable sadness at leaving the FIAT behind. Over the last two weeks, it had become a significant part of our Italian odyssey. We had, in no small way, become attached to it. I don't know if I will ever be able to look at an automatic transmission with satisfaction again.

We settled our Hertz bill. The cost was about 1200 Euros. Was it worth it? We think so. It cost, roughly, one hundred euros a day which paid for an unprecedented freedom that would be hard to duplicate with other transportation means. But now, we must play a wait-and-see game with the pernicious road cameras of the Italian poliziotto. Recall that Sophia took us to at least a few naughty places, so time will tell what other costs are involved with the FIAT.

We now proceeded to the terminal at the airport. We had plenty of time so we were not at all phased by getting ourselves stuck in a wrong line. We eventually found the correct line, got our boarding passes and went through security with the usual commotion and inconvenience.

We got to our gate and collapsed into the chairs. What had we just done? Did the last thirteen days really happen? An amazing calm came over us. Although our dream trip was over, we knew its memories would be with us for a very long time. The last few weeks whizzed by our eyes in a blur as we realized all that we had accomplished. To celebrate what seemed, at least to us, as a remarkable achievement, we got rid of some of our spare Euro coins by

Illustration 146: We made it!

purchasing two final gelatos.

Falling Onto Boston

The flight to Boston was uneventful but dreadfully long. I actually watched a whole movie; something I have never done on a plane. But, my other time was spent between dozing and watching the airline display of where the plane was positioned over the Atlantic Ocean.

After an eternity, we landed in Boston and went quickly through customs. There at the luggage carousel was our wonderful daughter, Sally, waiting to give us a personal ride to "Home Sweet Home". She was certainly a sight for sore eyes. We collected our baggage and were on our way through the "Big Dig". Merging onto I93 put us in perfect position for the ride home.

The house was still standing. As we expected, the grass needed cutting. The house had a thirteen day unused smell as we went through the door, but it disappeared quickly as we opened a few windows letting in a little fresh New England air. We had made it.

We were certainly glad to get home, however, I must admit that now, as I write these final words some two months after our trip, a very large part of my heart is still in Italy and I'm not at all certain that it will ever return to the US with me.

Epilogue

We get a lot of questions about our Italian genealogical odyssey. Many of these questions involve our use of a rental car as as a means of transportation. People want to know if we would have been better off using trains and buses. A lot of folks wonder how wise it was that we undertook the trip without a paid guide. The single question we get most is, "Would you do this trip again, the same way?" I can't describe to you how fast the word, "yes" forms in my brain, leaps through some nervous system to my tongue and is uttered from my mouth. As fast as you would hear, "Yes", come out of my mouth, it would come out of Gay's mouth a split second faster.

Our little FIAT 500 allowed us to go where we wanted to go, when we wanted to go. It got us to the places we needed to go and allowed us to take side trips to interesting sights and places. Having the comfortable and surprisingly roomy FIAT played more than a small part in our successful odyssey.

We really, really, enjoyed this trip. The reality is that if we had unlimited funds, we would probably do trips like this every few months. You see, we think we accomplished a lot on this journey. We saw new things. We saw beautiful things. We met good people. We made lifelong friends. We enjoyed fresh and delicious food. We experienced the culture of Italy and its Italians. And, oh, yes, we made a number of genealogical discoveries.

Yet, at the same time, we uncovered numerous avenues that have been left unexplored. There is so much more to do, and so precious little time to do it in.

There are more records to be found. There are more churches to explore. There is more family out there that we would love to meet.

Don't be lulled into thinking that the only object of this trip was to gather genealogical facts. That would be a sad misrepresentation of the experiences that captured our hearts along the way.

Do you want to see kind people? Do you want to see curious people? Do you want to see concerned people? Do you want to see a loving people? Do you want to see a proud people? Do you relish an intangible emotional high that will result in a deep and lasting satisfaction. Follow our footsteps. It doesn't need to be Italy. There are wonderful loving people worldwide.

Here, some seven months after our odyssey, we can't believe the detail we are able to recall about each and every day of our adventure, thanks in part to the great notes that Gay took while I was struggling with internet connections and an Italian speaking GPS. But also thanks, in a large way, for the human propensity to make room in the brain for significant memories. If we were to record everything we remember, here, in this book, it would be unreasonably long. Here, instead, is a quick summary of many of the things we consider accomplishments:

Avellino
- We met and received great help from an accomplished genealogist, Joe DeSimone.
- We met our Facebook cousin Pellegrino Mascolo and had a wonderful dinner with his parents
- We saw two old family churches
- We collected several family records at the Avellino Archivio di Stato.

Sassano
- We found the Sassano cemetery
- We made new friends while touring the old town on a hill
- We met with Don Otello Russo and found a remarkable marriage certificate, partially in Latin
- We visited the Museum Del Cognome in Padula and met with Mormon genealogist Michele Cartusciello
- We retrieved several records from the Ufficio di Anagrafe
- We met with Facebook cousin Oreste Barbella and his family

Palo Del Colle
- We attended a festival and toured the city with, now lifelong, Facebook friends, cousin Vito Tricarico and his family
- We stayed on a wonderful farm with Marie and Domenico Vero
- We saw the Palo del Colle cemetery
- We got a personal tour of Giovinazzo and Bari with Domenico Tricarico as our guide.

- We met a real cousin, Angela Lattanzio
- We retrieved some useful records from the Trani Archivio di Stato

Vasto

- We saw ancestral churches
- We were shown Foglio di Famiglia by a wonderful clerk in the Vasto Ufficio di Anagrafe
- We found more records in the Chieti Archivio di Stato
- We learned how to make "Wine Cookies"
- We stayed at Brunetta and Bepe's wonderful agriturisimo, Rifugiomare.

Put all this together with making dozens of new friends, visiting old friends, and seeing so many wonderful sights and you might gain a sense of how satisfied we are and how little we regret taking the trip the way we did.

Regrets are terrible things. They are like excess baggage that we must carry, sometimes for a lifetime. You should live your life avoiding regrets like the plague. Taking this trip is one thing we will never have to worry about regretting.

Ne Vale La Pena

Peter and Gayann Tricarico Barbella
November, 2014

The following appendices comprise, for the most part, verbatim translations of the many historical plaques that we we had the privilege to see on our trip. The last (but certainly not the least) appendix provides the recipe for the delicious wine cookies that Rifugiomare introduced us to.

Appendix I

Giovinazzo

The village rises on top of a promontory, stretching out towards the sea. It has ancient origins, even though its exact foundation period is uncertain. According to legend, the founder of Jovis natio was Perseus, son of Jupiter. Reliable pieces of evidence date back to the IXth century, where the city is referred to as a diocese. In 1257, Manfredi enfeoffed it to his cousin, Giordano Lancia, and in the XVIth century it became the estate of Ferdinando Gonzaga.

Giovinazzo conserves valuable historical and artistic evidence that dates back to various eras:
The Cathedral, built in the XIIth century in the typical Apulian Romanesque style and restructured various times, is flanked by two bell towers: one dates back to the Cathedral's original foundation, and the other to the seventeenth century. Behind the Cathedral, you can see the imposing Palazzo Ducale, built in the second half of the XVIIth century on request of Niccolò Giudice, Duke of Giovinazzo and Prince of Cellamare, according to a project

by the Neapolitan architect Francesco Antonio Picchiatti. The building unfolds around a big inner courtyard, and the northern facade rises on the ancient defense walls. Palazzo Lupis, also known as "Forlocco", dates back to the XIIIth century. It used to be the residence of an ancient, aristocratic family, the Luponi's, to whom the famous sixteenth-century poet and chronicler, Bisanzio Lupis, belonged. The Palazzo displays late Gothic elements on the ground floor and late Renaissance shapes on the upper floor. The family's coat of arms appears on the main facade: a wolf howling towards the sun. The Church of St. John the Baptist, formerly S. Maria dell'Episcopio (IVth century), was the village's first Bishop see. In 1174, it was dedicated to the apostles Paul and John, and in 1553 it was incorporated in the adjacent church of St. John the Baptist, known as St. John the Baptist "of the nuns", due to the nearby convent of the Benedictine nuns, built in the Xth century and largely destroyed at the end of the XIXth century. The church's bell tower hosts the city's oldest bell (1492). Palazzo Saraceno is one of the best examples of a Renaissance residence of the XVth century. One of its peculiar elements is the bugnato podium that greatly projects from the main facade. The various elements that can be seen on the outside (coats of arms, inscriptions, the Renaissance window and the gateway) show Catalan influences. The Church of the Holy Spirit, built on request of Bishop Pavone Griffi in 1395 displays late Romanesque shapes and is characterized by the so-called "chiancarelle" system (stone slabs placed on top of each other, typical of the "trulli "): cupola roofings covered by a polygonal dome with a pyramid-shaped roof. The simple and charming Church of S. Maria degli Angeli, was built in the XIIth

century near the Norman walls, on the edge of the ancient
village, from which its popular name derived, S. Maria de
lo muro (St. Mary of the Walls), which was rebuilt with a
single nave and interesting frescoed medallions in the
XVIIth century. The Church of St. Mary of Constantinople,
that dates back to 1528, rises on the place where the ancient
aristocratic seat once was, and before a pagan temple
dedicated to the goddess Minerva. Formerly dedicated to
St. Rocco, it conserves a niche on the facade with a big
statue of the Saint, accomplished by the sculptor A. Altieri.
On the inside one can admire the canvas paintings of C.
Rosa and Gieseppe and Saverio de Musso. Outside the
ancient village, passing through the Trajan Arch, decorated
with milestones of the ancient imperial road, you arrive to
the broad Piazza Vittorio Emanuele - the heart of the city -
embellished by a beautiful fountain with tritons,
accomplished by the sculptor T. Piscitelli. The Church of
St. Dominic and the adjacent monastery of the Dominican
Fathers (that became the "Royal Hospice Ferdinand I" for
the provinces of Bari and Otranto in 1819) face the piazza.
The building of the church began in 1704, according to the
neoclassical style, by the Dominican Father Antonio
Cantalupi, and was only completed in 1885. The church
hosts the valuable painting of St. Felix on the Chair, by
Lorenzo Lotto (1542) and canvas paintings of the brothers
Giuseppe and Saverio di Musso. A special tribute goes to
the Church of the Eternal Father, former church of Santa
Maria di Corsignano, built in the XIIth century in the
countryside around Giovinazzo. Another monument
worth mentioning is finally the Dolmen of St. Sylvester,
that rises in the homonymous village: a typical example of
a megalithic tomb of the Bronze Age.

Appendix II

Cathedral of Giovinazzo

Situated to the extreme north of the historic centre, the Cathedral of Giovinazzo is dedicated to St. Mary of the Assumption to Heaven. On the 6th December 1113, Princess Costanza of France, widow of Prince Boemondo Ist of Altavilla, in remembrance of her husband, donated the sum of money required to build it to the clergy. The Church was finished in 1180 and consecrated on the 20th May 1283. Built along lines of San Nicola di Bari, its original groundplan was in the style of a basilica with apses enclosed in the wall to the east. With three naves and a transept, it was subject to considerable alterations over the centuries with changes and superimpositions in the Baroque manner. Of the early Romanesque style of Puglia only the crypt has survived and the the southern facade with a very fine doorway decorated with a rich vaulted arch surmounted by a pediment which encases a low relief depicting the mystic lamb. From the XVIIth to XVIII cents. The longitudinal body of the Church was demolished, enlarged and rebuilt in its present form. In 1893, in replicas of the ones there before, the architect E. Bernich reworked the southern facade of the transept, the rose windows surrounded by animal figures, the large two bay window and the motif of the entwined arches. Of considerable interest is the apse section with its intertwining arches, two single bay windows, two small lozenge shaped windows, two double bay windows with

moon shaped round arches, a third single bay window
with two lions holding up a further two stylised lions.
This part is narrow standing between two bell towers: the
left one has conserved its Puglian style Romanesque forms
while the other shorter one was rebuilt in the XVIIIth cent.
and houses the "bombaun", the nickname given to the
Cathedral's larger bell because of its solemn chimes.
Access is gained to the Church interior from the right hand
side by means of a double staircase, the Church being
about three metres above street level. The central nave and
the transept are covered by three low domes alternating
with cross vaults. On the main altar stands a silver
aedicule made in 1897 to a design by Bernich which houses
a venerated Bysantine icon of the Virgin and Child, known
as the Madonna of Corsignano, brought to the Cathedral in
1677 by members of the Corsignano. To the rear of the
altar the entire surface of the apse is covered with XVIIth
cent. paintings by Carlo Rosa. Recent restoration work
have brought to light in the Presbytery area fragments of
the ancient mosaic floor datable to between the XIIth and
the XIIIth cents. and, on the right hand wall, XVth and
XVIth cent frescoes. On the right pillar of the Presbytery
may be admired a panel painting with gilded background
portraying Christ the Redeemer, by an unknown painter
(XVth cent.) In the side naves there are three chapels on
each side. Worthy of note is an altar of the Holy Sacrament
in polychrome marble, a work by C. Trinchese; a wooden
crucifix of the XIVth cent. (known as the "Daccoro"
Christ); the XVIth cent. icon of the Madonna of Grace by
the Puglian painter L. Palvisino; the gilded wooden bust
by the Neapolitan School portraying the Blessed Nicola
Paglia; the monumental XVIIIth cent. organ attributed to

Pietro di Simone and, last of all, some fine paintings by the De Musso brothers. From the left nave one may descend to the beautiful crypt, completed in 1150, surmounted by cross vaults and held up by 10 columns of different periods with Romanesque capitals. The Church conserves further fine treasures including a cross - a silver inlaid reliquary of the XVth cent. and an ivory Byzantine chest of the XIth cent. The archive of the diocese is very full and houses a great many parchment manuscripts, books, registers and paper documents.

Appendix III

The Ducal Palace of Giovinazzo

The Ducal Palace of Giovinazzo was built in the mid-XVIIth cent. at the wish of Nicolo Giudice, the Duke of Giovinazzo and Prince of Cellamare, to designs by Francesco Antonio Picchiatti of Naples, an architect to the Court of many talents. The building later became owned by the Sicilian Marquises of Rende, who lived there for quite some time. The building rises around a large inner courtyard over an area of approximately 500 sq. meters and has long, imposing facades made of squared blocks of stone. The northern facade was built on top of the ancient town walls, as may be seen from the wedged walling in the lower section, and looks straight out to the sea. What is visible today is entirely different on account of a road built for the pier which interfered with the building's earlier connection to the coast. An elegant balcony extended all along this side of the building, pierced by a series of French windows. This balcony, made of cut stone with shaped balustrades and ledges, would, with its effects of chiaroscuro, have lent the facade and indeed the entire building, a distinctly monumental character. Of this lovely belvedere, now almost entirely collapsed, only a few ledges and windows can now still be admired. The second floor of this wing of the palace also collapsed and has now been replaced with terraces. At the end of the south side once rose two towers but only a reconstruction of the eastern one and the lower part of the one to the west are now left. The southern facade contains an elegant entrance doorway, of clearly Catalonian influence; framed in by pilasters of alternating ashlars it imposingly extends well above the floor-marking cornice of the whole facade. The doorway chambers is covered by a notched barrel vault and to the right stands a double stairway, covered with a barrel vault, leading up to the floors above which comprise about a hundred different rooms. In the centre of the vast courtyard stands a well where rain water collected. The ground floor was articulated with a series of arches, now filled in, whereas on the two upper floors are two levels of French windows. On the master floor there were great reception rooms covered with lunetted pavilion vaults that were split up by partitioning walls over the years.

Appendix IV

Francis of Assisi

This plaque, placed in May of 1927 commemorates the 700th year from the death of the patron saint of Vasto, Francis of Assisi

Appendix V

Palazzo Siciliano – Marchese di Rende

The residence of the Siciliano family was built in the mid-XIXth cent. in late Neoclassical style to designs by a local architect named Giovanni Mastropasqua. It was built over the site of the former Church of St. Martha and with its facade still makes a very fine piece of scenery in the stylish Corso Principe Amedeo.

The base section of the facade is fashioned in elegant ashlarwork while the two upper floors are articulated with long slim Ionic half columns with ridging. The balconied windows on the first floor have alternately triangular and curving pediments.

After going through the vestibule and crossing through an ornate courtyard, all around the perimeter, of Tuscan, composite and Corinthian order pillars, one comes to the rooms of the Palace itself. A stairway with two flights of steps leads up to the master floor where there are lovely rooms with pavilion-style vaults, some of which still have their original floors made of white and black enamelled terracotta. The central hall has unfortunately been divided into two parts.

Also the small chapel still has its original floor of enamelled terracotta with the emblem of the Siciliano di

Rende family in the middle: a pine tree with two lion rampants at the sides. The emblem is surmounted by the crown of the Marquises. The chapel's dome with a small lantern above can be seen from the palace vestibule.

Cardinal Camillo Siciliano had Giacomo della Chiesa, the future Pope Benedict XVth, as a guest in this residence.

Appendix VI

Cattedrale Di San Giuseppe - Vasto

Tradition has it that today's Cathedral was built in the 13th century at the wish of Count Rolando Palatino and dedicated to Santa Margherita. The doorway, sculpted in stone, is datable to the original phase of building, crafted in Romanesque style by Master Ruggero de Frageniis in 1293. Next to the Church building is the monastery of the Order of the Augustinians, and it was here that in 1266 the Beato Angelo da Furci took on the habit of the Augustinians and stayed until 1271, when he set out on his journey to Paris to perfect his theological studies.

As with many buildings in the town and along the entire coast of Abruzzo, this church, on the 1st of August, 1566 was burnt down by the Turks in one of the most dramatic moments in the area's history. A devastating attack took place while 105 Moslem galleons, proceeding towards an attack on Venezia, wreaked death and destruction all along the coast. During the sack, the Cathedral of Vasto was completely destroyed, leaving only the facade with the rose window. Rebuilding work was begun in 1568 on the part of the Prior of the Monastery, Frate Angelo da Vasto. The Baroque bell tower is datable to 1730.

In the 17th century the Church was dedicated to St.

Augustine as it was annexed to an Augustine monastery and it was not until 1808, after the suppression of the Orders, it was given its present name in honour of St. Joseph to celebrate Joseph Napoleon, who at that time was ruling over the Kingdom of Naples. In 1853 it was promoted to the rank of Cathedral. In 1893, for safety reasons, the Church was completely rebuilt, except for the facade, to designs by Engineer R. Benedetti, who came up with a Latin cross structure in the Gothic revival manner. The composition of two-toned ribbing is a clever reinterpretation of style forms found in Medieval Tuscan buildings. In 1923 the interior was decorated throughout by the painter Achille Carnevali, while the ornamental scheme of the Chapel of the Sacred Heart was taken care of by the Canci firm. Notable works housed in the Church include a 16th century painting of St. Mary of the Sorrows, executed at the wish of Cola Bevilacqua in 1505 especially for the damaged chapel of the Cona a Mare, and a panel painting depicting the Baptism of St Augustine, datable to the 16th century and bearing the signature "Aloysius Benefactus, Pauli Veronensis nepos pinxit". Finally there are two very interesting sculptures, one of St. Augustine and the other of St. Monica, datable to the 17th century, and a rendering of St. Joseph, all restored when repair work was going on recently inside the Church.

Appendix VII

Wine Cookies

Ingredients

1 cup of sugar
1 cup of olive oil (or a little less, to taste)
1 cup of wine (red or white)
3 cups of flour
1 teaspoon of baking powder

Mix all the ingredients together into a pasty dough. Roll the dough, by hand, into small meatball size balls. Roll the balls in sugar.

Preheat your oven to 350 degrees

Place the balls on a cookie sheet and bake them for 20 minutes

This recipe is courtesy of Brunetta Bucciarelli of the agriturismo Rifugiomare.

About The Authors

Peter and Gayann Barbella are avid genealogists.   Both retired, they reside in New England with twelve of their thirteen descendants. Peter's Mom and Dad are American born Italians. He grew up in an Italian household in Tarrytown, New York. His first book, "27 Cottage Place" was published in 2013. It is a memoir motivated by the realization of how little he knew of his father's boyhood.

Gayann is half Italian and an esoteric mixture of English, Irish, and Dutch which gives her membership in the Daughters of the American Revolution and Descendants of the Mayflower. She is from Elmsford, New York, and often enjoyed the company of her Italian grandparents.

Peter and Gayann met in 1960 and were married in 1965. In forty nine years of marriage, they have received more than their share of God's blessings.

Besides genealogy, they enjoy music, theater, golf, exercising, and a hideaway on Cape Cod.

List of Illustrations

Bibliography

Paolicelli, Paul. "Dances with Luigi", St. Martin's Griffin; 2001

Leonard, Mary Hall. "Mattapoisett and Old Rochester Massachusetts", Grafton, 1907

Kertzer, David. "Sacrificed for Honor: Italian Infant Abandonment and the Politics of Reproductive Control", Beacon PR, 1993

Nelson, Lynn. "Discovering Your Italian Ancestors", Betterway Books, 1997

Cole, Trafford R. "Italian Genealogical Records", Ancestry Publishing, 1995

Pucci, Idanna. "The Trials of Maria Barbella", Four Walls Eight Windows, 1996

King, Ross. "Michelangelo and The Pope's Ceiling", Pimlico, 2006

Tricarico, Vito. "Erculea Proles", Cultura Fresca, 2012

Barbella, Peter. "27 Cottage Place", CreateSpace, 2013

Kittel, Eli Sumner Wetmore,"The Ketel Family",The University of Wisconsin - Madison,1946

Weise, Arthur James. "The Ketelhuyn Chronicles", Trow Directory, 1899

Hammond, Roland. "A History and genealogy of the Descendants of William Hammond of London, England", Boston: David Clapp & Son, Printers, 1894

Alphabetical Index